chartered
management
institute

inspiring leaders

business
PLANS

DAVID LLOYD

D0265705

Hodder Arnold

A MEMBER OF THE HODDER HEADLINE GROUP

To Edward, Oliver, Freddie
With huge gratitude to Eileen

The publisher has used its best endeavours to ensure that the URLs for external websites referred to in this book are correct and active at the time of going to press. However, the publisher and the author have no responsibility for the websites and can make no guarantee that a site will remain live or that the content will remain relevant, decent or appropriate.

Orders: Please contact Bookpoint Ltd, 130 Milton Park, Abingdon, Oxon OX14 4SB. Telephone: (44) 01235 827720, Fax: (44) 01235 400454. Lines are open from 9.00 to 5.00, Monday to Saturday, with a 24-hour message answering service. You can also order through our website www.hoddereducation.co.uk.

British Library Cataloguing in Publication Data
A catalogue record for this title is available from the British Library.

ISBN-13: 978 0340 94650 3

First published in UK 2007 by Hodder Education, 338 Euston Road, London NW1 3BH in association with the Chartered Management Institute.

Typeset by Transet Limited, Coventry, England.
Printed in Great Britain for Hodder Education, a division of Hodder Headline, an Hachette Livre UK Company, 338 Euston Road, London NW1 3BH by Cox & Wyman Ltd, Reading, Berkshire.

Hodder Headline's policy is to use papers that are natural, renewable and recyclable products and made from wood grown in sustainable forests. The logging and manufacturing processes are expected to conform to the environmental regulations of the country of origin.

Impression number   10 9 8 7 6 5 4 3 2 1
Year   2012 2011 2010 2009 2008 2007

The Chartered Management Institute

The Chartered Management Institute is the only chartered professional body that is dedicated to management and leadership. We are committed to raising the performance of business by championing management.

We represent 71,000 individual managers and have 450 corporate members. Within the Institute there are also a number of distinct specialisms, including the Institute of Management Consultancy and Women in Management Network.

We exist to help managers tackle the management challenges they face on a daily basis by raising the standard of management in the UK. We are here to help individuals become better managers and companies develop better managers.

We do this through a wide range of products and services, from practical management checklists to tailored training and qualifications. We produce research on the latest 'hot' management issues, provide a vast array of useful information through our online management information centre, as well as offering consultancy services and career information.

You can access these resources 'off the shelf' or we can provide solutions just for you. Our range of products and services are designed to ensure companies and managers develop their potential and excel. Whether you are at the start of your career or a proven performer in the boardroom, we have something for you.

We engage policy makers and opinion formers and, as the leading authority on management, we're regularly consulted on a range of management issues. Through our in-depth research and regular policy surveys of members, we have a deep understanding of the latest management trends.

For more information visit our website **www.managers.org.uk** or call us on **01536 207307**.

Chartered Manager

Transform the way you work

The Chartered Management Institute's Chartered Manager award is the ultimate accolade for practising professional managers. Designed to transform the way you think about your work and how you add value to your organisation, as it is based on demonstrating measurable impact.

This unique award proves your ability to make a real difference in the workplace.

Chartered Manager focuses on the six vital business skills of:
- Leading people
- Managing change
- Meeting customer needs
- Managing information and knowledge
- Managing activities and resources
- Managing yourself

Transform your organisation

There is a clear and well-established link between good management and improved organisational performance. Recognising this, the Chartered Manager scheme requires individuals to demonstrate how they are applying their leadership and change management skills to make significant impact within their organisation.

Transform your career

Whatever career stage a manager is at Chartered Manager will set them apart. Chartered Manager has proven to be a stimulus to career progression, either via recognition by their current employer or through the motivation to move on to more challenging roles with new employers.

But don't take just our word for it ...

Chartered Manager has transformed the careers and organisations of managers in all sectors.

- *'Being a Chartered Manager was one of the main contributing factors which led to my recent promotion.'*
  Lloyd Ross, Programme Delivery Manager, British Nuclear Fuels

- *'I am quite sure that a part of the reason for my success in achieving my appointment was due to my Chartered Manager award which provided excellent, independent evidence that I was a high quality manager.'*
  Donaree Marshall, Head of Programme Management Office, Water Service, Belfast

- *'The whole process has been very positive, giving me confidence in my strengths as a manager but also helping me to identify the areas of my skills that I want to develop. I am delighted and proud to have the accolade of Chartered Manager.'*
  Allen Hudson, School Support Services Manager, Dudley Metropolitan County Council

- *'As we are in a time of profound change, I believe that I have, as a result of my change management skills been able to provide leadership to my staff. Indeed, I took over three teams and carefully built an integrated team, which is beginning to perform really well. I believe that the process I went through to gain Chartered Manager status assisted me in achieving this and consequently was of considerable benefit to my organisation.'*
  George Smart, SPO and D/Head of Resettlement, HM Prison Swaleside

To find out more or to request further information please visit our website **www.managers.org.uk/cmgr** or call us on **01536 207429**.

Contents

CHAPTER 02

CHAPTER 03

CHAPTER 04

PEOPLE: HOW DO I SHOW THAT I (AND THE PEOPLE AROUND ME) HAVE WHAT IT TAKES? 48

CHAPTER 05

CHAPTER 06

CHAPTER 07

THE FINANCES: HOW DO I LEARN TO UNDERSTAND THE NUMBERS AND USE THEM TO SUPPORT MY BUSINESS CASE?

CHAPTER 08

CHAPTER 09

CHAPTER 10

HOW DO I AVOID THE MOST COMMON BUSINESS PLAN PITFALLS?

APPENDICES

INDEX

Preface

Producing a professional business plan will give your business the very best chance of success. This step-by-step guide covers the essentials for writing a compelling plan, by combining leading management theory with practical tips for making the whole process as streamlined as possible.

The starting point for your business plan is you, the individual manager. The process of preparing that plan is a personal development exercise in itself, making the business planning process doubly worthwhile, since it represents time invested in your business and in your own business skills.

How? When your business plan is complete you will have analysed your business's marketplace and assessed its rivals, gained a comprehensive understanding of customers' needs, faced squarely the business forces that drive profitability in your business's industry, decided upon financial targets, and identified the resources that your business needs to achieve its goals. And all within a context of gaining an understanding of your own business strengths and weaknesses.

In short, you will have completed an intensive management development programme.

David Lloyd

01

Why is a business plan so important?

We live in a moment of history where change is so speeded up that we begin to see the present only when it is already disappearing.

R. D. Laing

The past is a foreign country, they do things differently there.

L. P. Hartley

Introduction

This book provides clear and practical guidance about how to produce a top-quality business plan, and explains leading management thinking from the perspective of the real world. For anyone occupying an entrepreneurial role, whether in the private or public sectors, large company or small, as employee or self-employed, a business plan makes business life a lot more secure because, quite simply, it reduces business risk.

This chapter is all about starting with the correct perspective, understanding about the process of business planning rather than diving straight into it.

Everything changes

Few things are certain in business, which is why it is such an exciting place in which to operate. There is another side to that uncertainty however, the hard business reality of constant change, sometimes rapid, sometimes almost imperceptibly slow, but always present.

Change is a constant of business life, and is faced by all enterprises from the smallest start-up to the largest and longest-established company. Every successful business must embrace change to keep moving forward as it meets new customer needs, and evolves and changes itself in the process. Standing still is merely an illusion for the unwary, for really it means going backwards.

If the past is a foreign country, then the future is another yet. On entering new terrain a traveller can stumble around in the hope that something turns up before they perish, or progress safely by obtaining a map and choosing the safest path. In business terms, the best way to secure that map and select the route that leads to your desired destination is to put together a robust business plan.

The route to success in business invariably presents many challenges, and without a business plan it will be a journey without a map. Once you have that map, however, your business' present position can be established and you can then set out with confidence towards your chosen objectives. Your business plan will also let management measure progress and identify the resources that have to be secured at each stage.

Stacking the odds of success in your favour

Whether you are running an existing business that is aiming for growth and expansion, starting a brand new one, or acquiring an established business or a business franchise, preparing a business plan stacks the odds of business success in your favour. By changing the odds, the act of devising a formal plan considerably improves your business's chances of success; this book will show you how to prepare one well.

The fundamental principles of good business planning are equally valid for all businesses, from the smallest start-ups to the largest long-established companies, from one-person companies to multiple-generation family businesses, for service businesses and for product-based businesses, from low-tech to hi-tech.

This book draws upon three decades' experience of observing and advising hundreds of successful businesses. The ideas and the proven business planning techniques that it explains are designed for entrepreneurs, for experienced and newly promoted managers, and not least for business people with years of experience, whether or not they have previously received very much business training.

Providing a framework

In business, the perspective is generally one of partial insights and glimpsed opportunities, surrounded by factors that are uncertain, not easily controllable, and in some situations unknowable. The odds are stacked against success, in fact. There are always many more ways for things to go wrong than for them to go right. The role of all business plans is to provide structure in that situation, imposing order and a workable framework for rational and consistent decision-making by management.

Every business has objectives and values, explicit or implicit. These will have been set as the result of careful consideration, or they may perhaps simply have evolved over time. All businesses have processes that require management review and control, and most need to bid for scarce funding resources, whether from outside investors and bankers, or from internal corporate budgeting and bidding processes. Every businesses has blind spots, and all face the unknown. Preparing a business plan puts you more in control, gives you more controls in fact, more ways of shaping events and seizing the opportunities that arise.

For your business and for you

Preparing a strong business plan will require a significant commitment of time, that scarcest resource for the busy manager. However, out of that investment of time for your business will also flow learning opportunities and personal development benefits. Decide to see the time you spend as time invested in yourself. This important aspect of business planning is not always appreciated. Producing an excellent business plan may be your primary objective, but the potential benefits accrue not only to your business but also to you personally as author of the plan.

In addition, when your business plan explains your business in a compelling way, it will also highlight your own abilities as it does so. That means that your chances of successfully communicating your business ideas to others, and of winning their support, will increase enormously. People will buy into the whole business package because it rings true; the business concept as set out in your plan will dovetail exactly with the person that they see in front of them.

The wise and the cynical know that there are no certain routes to success in business, no infallible get-rich-quick schemes, but there certainly exist tried and tested ways of developing and exploiting your business's critical competitive edge. Television has brought to many people's consciousness a world in which would-be entrepreneurs seek to persuade experienced and hard-nosed businesspeople to invest in fledgling business concepts. Few succeed. Such programmes are good spectator sport of course, but are also rather instructive.

During many of the presentations, the pitches by the hopefuls, flaws emerge. Some are fatal, some not. The weaknesses may lie within basic business concepts and/or in the business skills of the individuals behind them. Yet those issues should have become visible when drawing up a business plan, and would have been addressable at that point. Everyone's task would be much simpler if they had invested time in producing a thorough business plan.

Why business plans work

In that context, here is the first helpful dose of reality. Business planning is in fact not about getting everything right all of the time. That is an unattainable goal, something that perhaps needs saying more often. It is instead about using your skills to maximise the resources available. It is about playing the percentages, about knowing that you will be wrong sometimes, but adopting a learning approach that will ensure over time that you will be a lot more right. Most of all it is about being more right than your competitors when it comes to understanding your customers' needs and exceeding their expectations.

There is a Japanese proverb that says that if you fall down seven times, stand up eight. After advising many hundreds of businesses over the last 30 years, I can identify only a single factor that links all of them, the reality that they all made major mistakes. The element that distinguishes the successful ones, however, was their ability to learn from their errors, to keep adapting and changing, to keep trying new things out. They held on to what worked well, and improved it, and they discarded or changed the things that did not work. In other words, success lay in the management process, the fundamental ways in which the successful businesses operated.

The result was that on balance, over time, the successful ones learned to make far fewer mistakes than their competitors. None was ever perfect. This book is written from that reality. The ideas and techniques included here are the distillation of seeing why the businesses that worked, worked, and why others failed.

The pivotal reason that having a well-constructed business plan adds hugely to the likelihood of business success is not always fully appreciated. Producing a good plan will provide a framework that will help to ensure better business decisions, true. The quality of the thinking behind the plan certainly matters, of course it does. But the bottom line is that it is the *process* of business planning that makes the vital difference.

The real benefits arise, happily for the individuals concerned, from the management processes of reviewing and analysing, of examining options and alternatives, of looking at results and taking corrective action. Most of all, the benefits arise from thinking constructively about the business in a structured way.

In short, the act of preparing a good business plan is really one of creating a self-fulfilling prophecy. When done well it will make your business more outward looking, more resilient, and more focused on meeting the well-defined needs of its customers. The process ensures that management's time and creative energies are engaged and then concentrated, and that as a result business resources and processes all become targeted at the achievement of known, desired, future events.

The alternative, frequently often in businesses, is a short-term focused and energy-sapping process of fighting the fires that flare up every day in the workplace.

Planning is the opposite of that greater or lesser chaos, and it provides perspectives to see the directions from which change is emerging. It therefore allows people to deal with business problems before they become critical. A good business plan sets out the particular activities which are the right things for the business to be doing, business strategy, and doing those things in ways that maximise the chances of achieving desired objectives and minimise the likelihood of failure, business tactics.

Planning also forces managers to take time out, to prioritise what really matters, to determine exactly what the desired business objectives are, and to work out the very best route for achieving them.

Business plans as management workout

This book takes as a matter of course the reality that all managers have gaps in their business skills base, and gaps in their outlook. The following chapters, and the business planning process that they set out, will allow you to deal with your own blind spots in business terms. Those blind spots may exist at a technical skills level – understanding business finance better, for example. The blind spots may also relate to dangerously hidden dips in the view of the road ahead – not seeing a business from its customers' viewpoint being a very common one. Not sure? Then when was the last time that you contacted your own business anonymously and tried to be a customer? It is a very good test.

Frustrating as it seems to onlookers, some managers become addicted to the adrenalin rush of fire-fighting, learning to love seat-of-the-pants decision-making. Living on the edge provides thrills and spills, but it will never produce a sound long-term business. Something big will go badly wrong, the question is really only one of when.

The urge to remain caught up in chaos, in quick-fix fire-fighting business solutions, reduces when managers begin to realise that producing a workable plan for business success also benefits them. This dual benefit, to the business and to its management, is essential since the management team is necessarily the main delivery mechanism for the business plan. A business will stand or fall, succeed or fail, achieve what its owners require from it or become a nightmarish experience, depending upon management's willingness to move away from fire-fighting.

Business plan format

Most business plans follow a broadly similar structure. This book provides a suggested format for your own business plan, but the final product will be yours and yours alone. You will produce your own plan, just as in the end it will be your business skills that determine whether and to what degree your business succeeds.

Business planning guides sometimes state emphatically that theirs is the best style of business plan, and that 22 pages (or 25, or 30) happens to be exactly the optimal length. Such rules are doubtless correct from the author's particular viewpoint, since each is presumably explaining how to produce a business plan that would impress them. Yet each, of course, is simply expressing their own specific preferences. I have seen good plans that were no more than a dozen pages long, and I have seen good plans that exceeded 30 pages. Businesses vary, business plans vary.

Getting the right focus

Your business may need financial backing, either from outside sources, including investors and bankers, and/or internally through some form of budget bidding or investment project appraisal process. However, and whether or not you seek funding, your business plan's primary focus lies in setting out a map for the business.

By producing a map for the business, by devoting your scarce time to producing a business plan that plots a clear way forward, you will improve the chances of your business succeeding. By doing that the corollary is that you will automatically increase your chances of securing the funding that it needs. A business' funding need comes out of its business plan, it has to be that way around. A plan that focuses on the funding rather than on the underlying business is very unlikely to be a good plan.

Creativity versus disciplined decision-making

The business planning process gives you the chance to be innovative, to think outside of the existing constraints, and at the same time it then forces you to be disciplined, working within real-world boundaries of what is possible and what is not. Producing a business plan is essentially a creative process, generating and accommodating new ideas, and seeing existing situations from new perspectives, but one which must have its roots planted firmly in reality. That sense of reality, the art of the possible, is what shines out of the best business plans.

Thinking slightly laterally is essential, tempered by the fact that being in business is very rarely about taking huge leaps, making single large decisions that change the world. Being in business is much more about taking many small steps, each one of which builds on the ones that went before in order to move things incrementally in a chosen direction.

The compounding of good business decisions is like that of compound interest in its cumulative effect, and over the course of time the results of the compounding process can become very impressive. Sound decisions, big strategic ones and smaller operational ones, all made within the context of clearly understood business objectives, will pile up on each other to build a sound and rapidly-growing business.

The most effective predator in the tropical rainforest is not the tiger, no matter how powerful any single individual animal is. The really effective predatory species is the army ants that sweep across the forest floor in broad columns, consuming everything edible in their path. Each individual insect effectively comprising a tiny part of a huge and hugely voracious predator.

The cascades of decisions needed to run any business are similar to armies of ants, small individually, but each contributing to a massive collective effect. Looking in from the outside, successful established businesses may most resemble individual large predators, but things are rarely as they appear. The underlying reality will be much closer to that of columns of ants, with many separate operating units, combining together, united in a determined pursuit of a shared plan, and operating within the context of known business objectives.

Continuing with an animal theme, there is an old joke about two hikers who round a bend on the trail to encounter 50 yards ahead of them a grizzly bear. As the first heaves off her rucksack and pulls on running shoes the second observes that she will never be fast enough to outrun the bear. 'But I don't have to outrun the bear my dear friend', replies the first, 'I only have to outrun you ...'

That story is an appropriate metaphor for the process of working towards business success. A never-ending stream of business decisions, better decisions piled upon earlier good ones, all made in order to keep you ahead of your rivals. The process of business planning allows you to keep stacking the odds in your favour so that you make many more right decisions than wrong ones, enabling you to make fewer mistakes than the competition. By being more alert than your rivals to what is happening, more open, more receptive, more willing to embrace change, you can ensure that whatever threats are out there on the business trail, you are more fleet of foot than they are.

Myths and legends

The techniques for successful business planning highlighted in this book have certainly been used many times by others, and viewing successful businesses as potential beacons of inspiration can be useful.

Being able to see an end result does not, however, mean being able to see the processes that led to that point of course. Be aware that it is not easy to look upon any established enterprise and easily identify correctly the evolutionary pathways that led to its present situation and condition. For example, WPP Group plc is one the world's largest media and communications groups, with a worldwide network of operations and revenues in 2006 of around £6,000 million. Yet the WPP name element relates to Wire and Plastic Products Limited, just one of many businesses in the family tree.

There also exists a temptation for entrepreneurs who head up successful businesses to re-write and maybe even polish their own histories to fit a desired script. This ex post facto rationalisation process is not uncommon, meaning that a company's history may be reinterpreted after the event to fit a certain desired version, quite possibly showing the founder bathed in a rosy glow.

Bear in mind then that history is rarely simple, and that it tends to be written by the victors after the vanquished have disappeared with little trace. Preserve a healthy scepticism when you hear tales about how successful businesses started and were then developed. Draw lessons where appropriate from others' stories, but always retain a small degree of caution and always be prepared to think for yourself.

The businesses that never were

This hardly needs saying, but for new ventures even the best business plans cannot on their own produce a successful business any more than a vat of picked grapes will produce bottles of claret. There are innumerable examples of excellent business ideas, worked up in the heads of able and energetic people, where the business plan itself somehow became the business. The individuals concerned, deep down, were not able for whatever reasons to take the step of actually going out and finding those first customers.

To succeed in business requires that you are determined to succeed in the real world, a place that is a very unforgiving taskmaster. Producing a business plan is a safe place in which to work out ideas and opportunities, and it can develop into a risk-free place of virtual business for its author. If the business planning process simply allows the would-be entrepreneur to stay out of the real world, to defer indefinitely the risks of rejection and of failure, then it will become an end in itself. That individual's business will never reach the starting line.

Your determination

If you have reached this point then the likelihood is high that you are committed to producing an excellent business plan for a strong and viable real world business. The most important word there is 'you'. The production of a top-quality plan will test your ability to make time, and your ability to marshal your thoughts in order to derive logical, sensible conclusions from them that will stand up to external scrutiny if needed.

In terms of your input, two factors are needed for success. The first has been mentioned already, forcing the planning process to happen by making enough space between your day-to-day fire-fighting activities to give yourself the time needed to plan. The second factor is directly related to that, your degree of determination.

Lack of determination sounds like it might be a problem that afflicts only new businesses, but it is not. A gradual weakening of focus most certainly affects existing businesses. The inertia of existing businesses often allows new entrants the space to set up and grab a slice of the action. To grow your business you must want to grow it, really want to grow it. It is not something that you can approach in a piecemeal way, or pick up and then put down again. Producing a plan will not, somehow, magically, make your business grow. Only you are able to do that.

Conclusion

Your business plan is about setting out the processes by which desired business objectives will be achieved, identifying the resources needed, and explaining how they will be marshalled. Producing a strong business plan will in itself maximise the chances of business success by focusing attention on supplying what customers really want, by identifying and addressing weaknesses, and by providing a clear route-map to show the way.

Business plans permit informed business decisions to be made in the light of the imperfect and incomplete data that is available, and the focus provided by a good business plan will ensure that the quality of those decisions is consistently higher than that generated by the stream of inconsistent and ad hoc decisions that is the alternative.

Wherever things stand for you at present, using this book to help produce your business plan will allow you to organise your thoughts within a bigger business framework, and to develop your ideas in a way that will give your business the very best chance. The challenge is to create order out of the fire-fighting and haphazard decision-making that will otherwise prevail. In business, as in life, there are many ways of getting things wrong, but very few of getting them right.

In the end, your business plan will be what you produce it to be, revealing the quality of your business concept and reflecting your own skills and ability. However, the process is a circular one, preparing a good business plan also enhances your management skills. You will not be producing a work of art, but when you complete your plan you should be able to take a degree of pride in it. If you don't feel that then something has gone wrong.

The chapters in this book themselves follow a standard business plan structure in order to provide you with a blueprint. Follow the blueprint and you will understand much better what makes your business tick. The next chapter starts the business planning process.

Tip

As you finish this chapter you may find it useful to scan the final chapter in this book, to ensure right from the outset that you are aware of the various areas in which many business plans go wrong. The sooner you understand where the major pitfalls lie, the easier they will be to avoid.

INSTANT TIP

Producing a strong business plan will in itself maximise the chances of business success by focussing management's attention on supplying what customers really want and providing a clear route map to show the way.

02

What do I need to do before writing a business plan and how do I get things started?

Chance favours the prepared mind.

Louis Pasteur

What you have to do ... is slow down ... whether you want to or not – but slow down deliberately and go over ground that you've been over before to see if the things you thought were important were really important and to – well – just stare at the machine. There's nothing wrong with that. Just live with it for a while.

Robert Pirsig, *Zen and the Art of Motorcycle Maintenance*

Introduction

Ironically the words 'I can't do that right now, I'm too busy' may be the most commonly heard excuses for not preparing a business plan. Those words reveal the Catch 22 situation that confronts all managers, that they are often too busy managing, sometimes frantic even, to take the time needed to manage well.

> ### Tip
> If you are waiting for enough time to become available to prepare your business plan then you will never have enough time, and if you think you are too busy to prepare a business plan then you *really* need that plan. The only variable is that some people will consciously decide to change they way that they run their businesses, whereas others will not.

This chapter is designed to help you get things started. It suggests starting by thinking about your business and about your own situation. Your business plan will benefit if you can see present circumstances through a fresh pair of eyes, and in doing so allow new perspectives to emerge. This is particularly true for existing businesses, where old thought patterns and habits can block new ideas, but is also valid for new businesses, where the quality of the final business plan can only be a direct function of the range and quality of ideas generated.

How to begin

As is true for so many things, taking the first step is often the most difficult. That first step is planning to plan, finding ways of taking time out from your normal day-to-day business activities in order to think and to start recording those thoughts. Only you can create that space, forcing it into your diary, and only you can remain determined not to move it subsequently.

At this point you may have many business ideas bubbling away, big strategic ones and essential but smaller-scale thoughts about operational issues. Your first task is to get those ideas fully recorded, and that means using a method that best suits your lifestyle. The best ideas often pop out in sideways situations, when your brain is relaxed and functioning without pressure.

Tip

Keep pen and notebook or electronic organiser with you at all times; a voice recorder is very useful too, especially in the car. Be able to capture your thoughts and ideas wherever they emerge, which certainly will not always be when you decide to focus specifically on your business plan.

Kick-start

The unique resource that your business possesses is you, and so identifying how things stand for you at present is a very shrewd starting point. In the end, the real bottom line is that the success or failure of your plan is your responsibility, and so getting to grips with your own situation most certainly matters.

To produce a compelling business plan you must be fully committed, since yours are the skills and motivation that will determine the quality of your plan.

Tip

The correct place to start is with you, everything else builds from there.

If you want to kick-start the whole process, you can begin by asking yourself these two questions from a business perspective:

- Where am I, right now?
- What factors about me led me to this point?

When thinking about those two questions, you are not trying to perform an in-depth personality assessment, nor writing your autobiography. Simply start by summarising briefly on a blank sheet of paper your career to date. Use bullet points, or boxes and bubbles, and identify the major factors which have led you to this particular point. Those factors will include external influences, of course, and personal choices.

Determine for yourself what makes most sense for your situation. You are trying to gain a sense of perspective about your own position, and also a degree of honesty with yourself about what you really want to achieve in business.

Self-reflection

As you take that reflective look at your present position, especially when you take the longer view of your business path to date, you are likely to see some patterns emerging, some consistencies in the ways in which you have approached things, and the choices that you have made in the past.

In the business planning courses with which I have been involved, the triggers that really started business owners and managers thinking, the events that began to make a real difference, were exercises that let them understand themselves better. This area is covered in more detail in Chapter 4 of this book, when the people aspects of your business are under the microscope.

For present purposes, the key point is that although we are each unique and no two individuals are, of course, ever the same, research shows that certain personality traits are shared by successful businesspeople. Your subjective self-appraisal here at the outset will help you to focus on this area later, what it is that makes you tick, since behavioural factors have a direct bearing upon the preparation of your business plan and indeed the future success of your business.

Chapter 4 outlines the types of personality test that are available to let you understand yourself more objectively in behavioural terms, and reveal which elements of your personality tend to match those of successful entrepreneurs, and which do not. In behavioural terms, your basic personality is augmented by your business experience and the management expertise that you have acquired over your career. Nature and nurture both play a part, and understanding your own personality traits in the context of your business will provide some illuminating insights.

Time spent reviewing your business motivations is also time well spent, revealing as it will just how committed you are to achieving your goals. One of the earliest thinkers in the field of business management, the late Peter Drucker, asked the really BIG question: if you are not in business for fun or profit, then what are you doing there? Either way, you will need to give 100 per cent commitment to your business to make it succeed.

Your business ambitions

In parallel with recognising your own situation, you need also to get a bearing on exactly what it is that your business planning need represents. The possibilities are many:

- Are you about to start out on your own? Do you have fresh ideas for a new business that are ready to go? Or are they presently at the initial concept stage?
- Do you run an established business that you wish to expand? Are you operating a business for someone else, with or without an ownership stake, possibly as the next generation of a family business, and want to change the way things work?
- Are you thinking of purchasing a business, or a ready-made business formula, a franchise?

Within those questions, the issue of size matters. Big can be beautiful, but small is beautiful, too. Are you aiming big or aiming small? Guides to business planning are sometimes framed in terms of larger business, ones that have or aim to have ambitions of national or even global presence. Yet the reality of 21st-century Britain is that smaller businesses taken together have a far greater effect on the economy as a whole than do the larger ones, the smaller ones create more employment opportunities, they generate more wealth, and they pay more taxes.

People set up every single day what are destined to become profitable local businesses. The founder's objectives may be modest, becoming big fish in small ponds perhaps, but they wish nevertheless to run their own enterprise. Your motivation may simply centre upon wanting freedom, the freedom to develop and grow a business, without any really big aspirations, at least not at present.

In real life, business ambition is normally quite modest. When you pause to think about it, it is doubtful that many of the founders of what are now global businesses started out with that level of ambition. Entry-level opportunities for new businesses always exist within smaller, localised markets, particularly in sectors that are quite fragmented. Examples include restaurants and hotels, alarm businesses and locksmiths, vehicle repairs businesses of various types, health salons, model shops, website designers, bookkeepers, minibus and taxi services, specialist building firms, and so on.

In other words, in industries where there are many relatively small businesses competing with each other, gaps in the existing offerings available to customers can often be identified, occupied, and turned into successful businesses. Those gaps may be geographical, but not always. Just doing things slightly differently to the competition is a key that can unlock so much, and the world being what it is, simply being better by doing what you say you will is often a very good start.

New entrants can and do set up successfully in fragmented industries when they are determined to deliver greater benefits to customers than the existing players. In such situations new businesses are rarely founded on new business ideas, instead the focus will be that of reformulating existing business ideas slightly, finding an angle that the existing players have overlooked or ignored.

Being determined to exploit rivals' complacency may seem arrogant, but successfully invading a fragmented local marketplace is often helped by a degree of inertia on the part of the competition. A fresh entrepreneurial spirit in a tired industry, welded to ability and determination, can carry a new business a very long way. Sometimes it takes a very long time even for the existing players to wake up and begin to notice what is happening.

Even in non-fragmented industries, and on a national scale, where only a few large and seemingly dominant players exist, new businesses may be able to exploit business opportunities. Larger companies may have decided not to bother with a particular market, or may not be able to exploit it profitably, or, again, maybe they have become a little complacent about customers' needs. The passage of time may have started to dull their customer focus, their competitive edge. Perhaps the competition is no longer trying quite as hard as it once did.

The essentials

This chapter is about getting things started, and the emphasis so far has been on you, the person behind the business. The next step is to start thinking about your business itself in big picture terms, and the first part of that is to understand clearly what it is that is needed in order for your business to succeed.

Building a successful business requires the following:

- Determination to succeed. Without that, nothing.
- That you identify and locate customer groups whose various needs your business's offering meets better than the competition's.
- That large enough numbers of those customers can be persuaded to purchase from your business at prices that produce enough profit to reward the effort and the level of risk involved.

Two of those statements focus upon the customer, the essential prerequisite to being in business. You must get that market focus very clear from the outset, since that perspective must stay visible throughout your business plan.

It all comes down to you, your skills and determination to shape your business's offering by various means so that it meets customers' needs better than any other. It is not about, most emphatically not about, trying to persuade customers that they really do need what your business happens to sell. If you go that way your business will eventually fail.

The big picture

Remember that you are not writing your business plan yet, you are preparing to write it.

You are investing thinking time at the outset, so that when you start writing the plan itself things become much simpler and almost certainly much quicker. Writing your business plan well will demand a bird's-eye view, an overview.

In terms of your business plan, thinking about your business itself in the biggest terms poses a challenge. At first, this may seem like an easy task, but you will find that as you start to consider the many issues that relate to your business, and the sheer width and depth of the factors that impact upon it, things become much more complicated.

Your task at this stage is to obtain perspectives that will give you that a whole panorama in due course. The big picture will include your views of the following rather daunting list:

- Your business's market(s) and customers and their attributes.
- The industry sector(s) in which your business operates, and its competitors.
- The resources that your business presently has available to it and the ones that must be secured.
- Your business's processes, how it operates.
- The many factors that impact upon your business, those that it can influence to a greater or lesser extent, and those which are largely uncontrollable.

In the real world, many people do not plan their business plans at all, choosing instead to dive right in and start writing. Adopting that approach leads to what had seemed to them, initially, as a straightforward task instead becoming a rabbit warren of openings and interlinked tunnels, with false entrances and many blind alleys. The result is that, as more and more confusion emerges, people become tempted to gloss over the more complex areas, the ones that do not slot easily into their thought processes. That process is the slippery slope towards what will probably emerge later as a business plan that contains some rather large gaps.

Visualise a funnel, very wide mouth at the top and a much smaller opening at the other end. Liquid poured in at the top circles to form a vortex, and what emerges at the other end of the funnel is a controlled outflow. So it has to be with the thought processes that lead to your business plan. Many ideas will flow into each other at the outset, ideas that need to be recorded and reformulated and polished during the business planning process. What will emerge in the form of the completed plan will be a controlled flow of processed ideas, all directed towards achieving your business's objectives.

Tip

You must be able to accommodate large numbers of ideas during the early planning stages. Those ideas need to stay visible and not be discarded too early or simply ignored in a misguided attempt to simplify things. An excellent way to take control of the recording of process is obtain some A3-sized sheets of blank paper, and create spider diagrams on them that record your thoughts. You can employ spider diagram software if you prefer.

The concept underlying spider diagrams is straightforward. They are a way of recording thoughts and ideas so that the linkages between them can be made diagrammatically, rather than using only written words. Each thought, each idea must be noted down within boxes or bubbles, known as 'nodes', and then links to other nodes and sub-nodes are indicated by using lines to join them up, creating a clear but rather untidy looking spider's web structure.

An example spider diagram is shown at Appendix A, and there are really few rules. This recording-of-ideas process is purposely not overly structured so that it allows freer associations and more creative thoughts to emerge, so certainly be creative. If you are doing your diagram manually, using blank paper, employ coloured pens, various nibs, straight lines and curved lines, dotted and curly lines, highlighter pens. If you are using any of the spider diagram-type software that is available, then experiment with it first to discover the options available to you.

> **Tip**
>
> There is a huge hidden bonus from using spider diagrams. As they take shape on the page, very gradually the first indications of order and structure will begin to emerge. Out of the diagram's meanderings, patterns and shapes will slowly make themselves visible to your brain. You will find yourself joining up distant nodes, seeing linkages that would have been very difficult to spot in a chunk of narrative.

The whole point of not using sequentially joined-up sentences is to help your brain to process its own thoughts. A picture is worth a thousand words, and spider diagrams, with their flexible linkages and connections, permit ideas to be set out and comprehended by the human brain far more flexibly than is the case if narrative alone is used. The words employed in a narrative can often lead the brain down already well-trodden pathways, which as a result may trigger fewer truly innovative ideas.

SWOT analysis

A spider diagram can provide an excellent means of recording your thoughts, but it should not be completed at a single sitting. Allow time in fact for as many of your ideas as possible to emerge, to evolve. Aim for several days' effort, at irregular intervals.

Once you think that your diagram is reaching a completion, for there will be no absolute stopping point, you can start produce another one, one that gathers together your thoughts and ideas in a more structured way. The example spider diagram already noted at Appendix A, is in fact an example of a second stage diagram, laid out in the form of a SWOT analysis.

SWOT is an acronym for the business analysis technique devised at Stanford University during the 1970s by a team led by Dr Albert Humphrey. The four SWOT headings supply the acronym and the framework to work within.

Strengths	**Weaknesses**
Opportunities	**Threats**

Figure 2.1

As part of the initial preparation process for your business plan, SWOT analysis can be a very helpful technique to let you sort out some of the complexity. You can use it to perform an overall business review. What are your business's strengths and what are its weaknesses? What are the opportunities and what are the threats lurk on the business horizon?

Performing a SWOT analysis allows you to analyse the big issues, and will help to impose organisation upon your thoughts about your business's present situation. Business issues will doubtless be visible in all business areas:

● Market(s) and individual customer groups.
● Competitors.
● People.
● Finances.

- Technical aspects of your product or service.
- Securing the supply of essential raw materials and specialised labour.
- Business processes.

The SWOT technique provides great flexibility, and it certainly lends itself readily to a group brainstorming approach. This can be from scratch, either as an adjunct to your own thought processes, or as a method in itself. If other key individuals are involved with your business, getting them to take part in an initial overall SWOT exercise can be an excellent way of enfranchising them. Use a flipchart or blank sheets of paper and encourage people's ideas and thoughts to flow, allowing the four headings to provide the triggers.

The aim is to get down as many ideas and thoughts as you are able to under each heading. Do not edit, do not censor. Focus people's efforts upon idea generation rather than getting too hung up about which heading best fits a given idea, since there will inevitably be overlaps. Your results can be reallocated between headings later, just as lines that link boxes in a spider diagram can be redrawn.

In any event, the fact that a given business strength may also a weakness in some respects may simply be the objective reality that confronts your business. It is far better to be aware of that situation. For a business that is subject to the whims of fashion, for example, having the most fashionable products for the time being will inevitably lead to concerns about the business's level of dependency upon rapidly shifting consumer tastes.

Tip

Use SWOT flexibly, not as a rigid straitjacket. See it as a process that allows thoughts to be marshalled into a clearer picture, which provides very useful insights. More creative results, and therefore the most useful ideas, emerge from SWOT when it is not treated as an exercise in which absolute precision is necessary. Very rarely does absolute precision exist in business terms.

PEST analysis

As noted at the start of this book, change is pervasive in business and serves to propel businesses forward. That change comes from outside and from within. Nations change and economies change, governments change and political policies change, employees change, technology changes, customers and competitors change, shareholders change. The world of business changes all the time, sometimes in great leaps, often in small steps, but the existence of change itself is a constant.

PEST, another acronym, is a technique commonly used in conjunction with SWOT to identify the major external factors for change that exert influence on business. Owners and managers focus inwards on their businesses as a matter of course, but are generally not so diligent about keeping under review the *external* environmental factors that affect those businesses. PEST enables management to look outwards at external factors, ones that are much less easily managed, some of which may appear also as threats in a SWOT analysis.

Time is a business resource, and it follows that the further ahead that warning signs of major external changes can be spotted, the better the chances for managers to handle them. External factors are by definition the more difficult to cope with. Business managers need to keep themselves aware of the existence of the major external influences upon their businesses, and of their potential effects,.

Appendix D shows the typical grid layout used for PEST analysis, with bullet point triggers. Use it as a prompt if you decide to run PEST as a group session. Using a spider-diagram to perform your business's PEST analysis also works very well.

The major PEST influences are as follows:

- **P**olitical influences: changes in national and in local governments, and their business-related policies.
  Examples include generally applicable legislation relating

to employment practices such as minimum hourly wage rates, anti-discrimination laws, health, safety and environmental regulation, and whole-industry regulation such as the Financial Services Act.

- **Economic influences:** the effects of national and international changes in the economic environment in which businesses operate. Examples include movements in interest rates, changes in people's levels of personal wealth, including changes in their perceptions of their levels of wealth and disposable incomes, and the consequent changes that occur in their willingness to spend money. People who feel positive tend to take bigger risks, and spend more money on luxury items, for example. Many people believe that the buoyancy of the UK housing market is a major influence, given the high proportion of homeowners in the UK.

- **Social influences:** cultural and sociological changes in society have a major impact on business. Changes, for example, in the age profile of the population, changes in the number of single-person households, changes in the average age at which children leave home, changes in the amount of people's leisure time, and indeed changes in their perceptions of what comprises a fair work-life balance, changes in numbers of individuals who work from home.

- **Technological influences:** the broad sweep of scientific and technological advance has always influenced business activity, most particularly since the Industrial Revolution. That advance has itself been driven by business endeavour, for the process is circular. Newly emerging and changing technologies exert a pervasive and accelerating effect upon business activities. Global mobile phone corporations could not have existed in 1980. Very few people in 1990 foresaw the arrival of the internet, but within a single generation it has fundamentally changed the way in which a large part of the world works.

PEST factors are pervasive in their effect, and although they relate to the bigger picture in business terms, they certainly have relevance for smaller enterprises as much as for larger ones. A village shop certainly feels the effect when more of its customers decide to drive to the nearest town to buy their provisions and, increasingly, a huge range of other products and services, from a supermarket. Conversely, an allotment holder can benefit from an upsurge in demand for organic produce grown locally and sold at farmers' markets, as more people decide to purchase loose vegetables locally from a market stall rather than buying pre-packaged ones flown in from another continent.

Just as with SWOT, overlaps between different PEST headings will happen. If personal or business tax rates are changed, or if the Chancellor introduces higher tax breaks for certain types of business expenditure, then both political and economic forces act together in ways that have a major impact upon business activity.

The four external influences assessed in a PEST analysis fit well with SWOT. The two analyses complement each other. As with SWOT, do not become overly concerned with making the boxes fit precisely, for what really matters are your thought processes and your confidence to be able to wield these techniques to gain new insights.

SWOT and PEST and your business plan

SWOT and PEST will furnish useful perspectives in due course when you start to prepare your business plan itself. By providing means of analysing the fundamental issues that affect your business, they also allow you to see other business elements in their true context, sat within the bigger picture.

Tip

Always start with the big issues and then move to the smaller ones. Do not try to contemplate fine details too quickly. The details matter, of course, they really matter, but to fit correctly into your business plan they must sit within the larger framework of your overall understanding about your business. SWOT and PEST techniques provide that framework.

Business plan appearance and length

As you begin to think about writing your plan proper, which starts at the next chapter, here are a few suggestions and guidelines to help frame your thoughts.

Your business plan must say what it needs to say succinctly; a good plan is certainly not measured by length or by weight. The next chapter addresses the first section, the Executive Summary, and how to use it to grab the reader's attention right from the outset. The rest of the plan must then hold it by keeping them interested and moving along, which means keeping the plan efficiently focused.

Tip

The first section of your plan should follow on from a professionally laid out contents page. Use triple spacing, allow daylight in to help the reader. It is a good idea also to rough out your plan's contents page at this stage, so that you have on paper and in your mind a vision about where your plan is going. Give your subconscious a map to work on.

Your business plan should be easy on the eye. Substance always matters more than form, but be aware that the fonts that you select do make a difference. Headings often stand out more if you use a streamlined-looking sans serif font, such as Arial or Verdana, and many people find that blocks of business text can appear more authoritative when a font with a serif is used, such as Times New Roman or Century Old Style.

In terms of length, and as a broad guide, each individual section of your plan might occupy two or three A4 sheets, indicating a completed document of perhaps 20 pages or so, excluding the appendices. Note, however, that individual business circumstances can always give rise to variations.

Tip

Leave a sufficient margin throughout your plan to allow readers to add their own notes. Your aim always is to make your businesss plan's format as helpful as possible for the reader.

Business plan software

It is worth mentioning business plan software. Business plan software packages seek to minimise the time needed to prepare a business plan, to streamline the process. Time is usually in short supply in business, but in reducing the time needed, a fine aim in itself, the risk is that software also reduces one of the main benefits of producing a business plan, the time spent in careful reflection and in original thought.

This is not to say that business planning packages lack merit. It is to say that using them tempts people under time pressure to take short-cuts. If the software provides a join-the-dots approach to planning, wholly or in part, and missing pieces are added to pre-set formulations, then the completed plan will almost inevitably lack depth of analysis. It will certainly lack originality, and despite possessing a superficial gloss the final product may end up feeling somewhat mechanised and formulaic.

Conclusion

Preparing a business plan well will require time and take energy, and preparing a good plan will take longer than preparing a weak one. If you really are serious about making your business succeed then you will find that extra time will turn out to be an investment that is repaid many times over.

You will be the author of your business plan, and it is your skills that will drive the business forward. For that reason, start your plan by thinking about your own position and motivation. That may sound like a step sideways, particularly if you are very busy, but it is actually a way of ensuring right from the start that you are fully tuned in your own commitment. You will certainly need to draw on that as you produce your plan.

After you have paused in order to establish what your own internal drivers really are, then start to think about your business. The management tools to use at this first stage, SWOT and PEST, allow you to analyse the bigger picture, make sense of great complexity, and distinguish between the many and interdependent factors that affect all businesses.

As your analyses develop, you will begin to see key issues emerging. Your business will be able to shape and influence some of those, whereas others although visible will be far less controllable.

When you have completed the first stage, the standing back and the calm analysis, you can begin to prepare your plan proper. Your familiarity with the big picture issues, the really key issues for your business, will ensure that you will always see things in the proper context. If you start your plan somewhere other, and d in at the detailed level is a very common mistake, then it becomes very difficult later on to draw back in order to obtain the correct perspective of your business as a whole.

INSTANT TIP

If you are waiting for enough time to become available to write your business plan then you will never have enough time and if you think you are too busy to prepare a business plan then you *really* need that plan.

03

How do I write an attention-grabbing Executive Summary?

'Million-to-one chances', she said, 'crop up nine times out of ten'.

Terry Pratchett, *Equal Rites*

Opportunity is missed by most people because It is dressed in overalls and looks like work.

Thomas Edison

Introduction

You are about to start on your plan proper, a document that is fundamentally designed to improve your business's chances of success. Producing a good plan takes effort, but to re-emphasise an earlier point, you should regard the time you devote to the task as an investment that will be repaid many times over.

Preparing your plan is a management-development exercise in itself. Learn to see it that way and it will become far more attractive as a prospect. Your goal is to produce a plan that does justice to your skills, and to your business's prospects, and which will drive the business forward towards stated, desired objectives.

An Executive Summary is really a business plan in a nutshell, a self-contained précis. In many respects it can be viewed as a front door, and your task is to write a stimulating summary that will make readers want to push that door open and step through into the plan itself. In terms of its length, simply place yourself in a reader's position, and respect their time. Since your Executive Summary should be exactly that, as a broad guide two A4-sized pages or so should be sufficient to cover the essentials.

Importance

The Executive Summary is the most important business plan section of all, drawing everything together right at the outset. It must be persuasive, and it needs to pack enough punch to hook a reader's interest and tell a compelling story that makes them interested enough to want to read the whole plan. If it fails in that, then no reader will ever go further. No one will find out how exciting your business concept is, or how competent you are.

For most readers of your business plan, business lives being what they are, your Executive Summary will have just one chance to do its job, probably less than five minutes of dedicated attention. During that very short time, the reader must decide whether to invest more of what is probably their own scarcest resource, time, in order to find out what the rest of the plan has to say.

Elevator pitch

An Executive Summary is a written version of what is sometimes referred to as an elevator pitch, quite simply a particular type of sales pitch. The idea is that it is should be possible to explain the key ideas and features of any business concept in no more than a minute or two. That is the timeframe of the undivided attention that would be available to you if you had managed to buttonhole a potential business partner or financial backer in a lift.

> ## Tip
> It is very easy to be too eager, to over-sell something and put the other person off by doing so. As a sales pitch, your summary has to sell your business idea, but although its tone will be a positive one, it must avoid hyperbole and exaggerated claims.

When to write it

By definition, the Executive Summary can only be written properly once the rest of your plan is substantially complete. The chapters in this book follow the recommended format for a business plan, which means that the Executive Summary is being covered at this point. However, having understood in broad terms what the Executive Summary section contains, and its crucial role for your business plan, you may decide at this point to move onto the next chapter.

> ## Tip
> Return to this point when you have completed the rest of your plan, at least to first draft stage, and are ready to make a start on the Executive Summary.

Areas to cover

Your business plan will marry narrative and the business numbers, since both are essential to make a strong business case. To make that case for your plan's Executive Summary, the following areas will need to be covered:

- Why the plan has been produced.
- Where funding is needed, a clear statement of what is required.
- An outline of your business and of its marketplace.
- Financial headlines.
- Thumbnail sketch of the key individuals involved.
- A statement of the business's goals.

Tip

Use non-technical language that is easy to understand, plain English. An intelligent, informed reader who is not a technical expert in your industry should be able to appreciate why your product or service will be successful.

To illustrate the point, here is an extract taken from the Executive Summary of a real business plan. It speaks for itself. Or, rather, it does not:

'[Software's] tools automate data integrity checking processes for spatial clashes, violations of the required data protocols, and random offsets within semi-static or discrete activity modes ... [Software's] knowledge-based digital components enable efficiencies in design and allow client value engineering to take place. In conjunction with procurement and cost handling data management systems [Software] provides the key enablers for re-engineering the critical time elements in the construction value chain.'

Words that are presumably full of meaning to the writer say almost nothing to the reader.

The Executive Summary's first specific task, often overlooked, is to summarise the reason for the business plan's existence, why it has been produced at all. Clarity at this point makes the reader's task as simple as possible, since they can appreciate right from the outset what the purpose of the plan is and, particularly in a funding context, understand exactly what is being asked for.

State clearly the main purposes of your plan, and highlight its role in the context of achieving the objectives of your business. As a minimum, that role will be one of setting out objectives, explaining your business's strategy and tactics for achieving them and providing a clear route-map.

Your summary should next explain in outline your business offering, the product or service being provided. Indicate briefly actual and potential markets, summarise who your business's customers are, highlighting particularly the customer problems that your business solves.

Tip

To produce a rapid prompt sheet to help you summarise your business's product or service, use a spider diagram. Take a blank sheet of paper and write down key words and phrases that describe in plain English the customer problems that the product or service solves.

Remember that you will be doing this summary after you have completed the rest of your plan, which should make the task rather easier. Then insert key words or phrases that describe how your business meets those customer needs, drawing in lines linking customers' needs to the ways in which your business meets them. Words that are comparatives like 'better looking', 'lower cost', 'faster', 'longer-lasting' should appear as the competitive advantages of your product or service begin to make themselves clear in the diagram.

A major purpose underlying the preparation of many business plans is a financial one, setting out the business case to secure long-term finance, or internal corporate funding, or shorter-term overdraft facilities from a bank. Your Executive Summary should state any finance need clearly and unambiguously. Once you have completed the Finance chapter of this book, you will understand the importance of securing the services of an accountant who communicates very well.

Tip

The finance section of your plan will furnish readers with the more details later, but your summary must contain the headlines.

Other headline financial information to include in summary form will be as follows:

- Forecast sales figures, together with recent sales history if your business is already trading.
- Forecast of trading profits and losses, together with historical profit and loss performance.
- Forecast net cash position, setting out the highest negatives in particular and explaining briefly the reasons for their existence.

The skills and experience of the main people involved in your business certainly matter, so next use a few sentences to provide the headlines about the key individuals. Tell the truth, of course, but focus on the relevant and the positive.

The Executive Summary should then outline the history and present ownership of your business, again in a few sentences.

Mission statements and goals

Some business plans include a formal business mission statement, encapsulating the basic purpose of your business. This might be contained in a single sentence, but will probably be longer. Including a mission statement can be a very useful way of ending your summary, uniting the separate business elements that exist in the context of your business plan. They are not universally popular, however, some people find them helpful, others think that they are bland at best.

Tip

If you do decide to develop a business mission statement, focus it upon the most basic reason for your business's existence. From that can then flow a summary of your business's goals, since these must be a function of the purpose of the business.

The easiest way to comprehend what mission statements do (or do not) do is to look at an example. The one below is from the website of Cadbury Schweppes plc (www.cadburyschweppes.com), but you will readily be able to locate others using the internet.

'What is your mission statement?
Our core purpose is working together to create brands people love. Our goals for 2004 to 2007 are:

- Deliver superior shareowner performance
- Profitably and significantly increase global confectionery share
- Profitably secure and grow regional beverages share
- Ensure our capabilities are best in class
- Nurture the trust of our colleagues and the communities in which we do business'

Figure 3.1

The Cadbury Schweppes website moves on to explain more about the company's goals and about its specific priorities within those goals, as follows:

'2006 goals and priorities

In October 2003, we set our strategic goals for the 2004–2007 period. Each goal has two priorities. While our goals are unlikely to change from year to year, the priorities may, depending on prevailing business needs and the market environment. The goals provide a small number of clear and achievable objectives against which our senior managers report and are incentivised.

In 2006, our goals remain largely unchanged. We have refined our fifth goal, building on our existing strong reputation with our employees and society, to focus on creating a cohesive and talented workforce, through encouraging inclusiveness and increasing the diversity of our people. We will continue to work to our high standards of corporate and social responsibility both in the way we conduct our business, and in our products and the way we sell them.

2004–7 Goals	2006 Priorities
1) Deliver superior shareowner performance	1) Deliver annual contract
	2) Execute 'Fuel for Growth' and focus on free Cash Flow
2) Profitably and significantly increase global confectionery share	3) Invest, innovate and execute
3) Profitably secure and grow regional beverages share	4) Leverage Smart Variety
	5) Invest, innovate and execute
4) Ensure our capabilities are best in class	6) Strengthen non carbonated drinks and route to market
5) Nurture the trust of our colleagues and the communities in which we do business	7) Embed core processes to improve business planning
	8) Focus on Supply Chain and transform IT
	9) Deepen talent pool and increase diversity and inclusiveness
	10) Continue high Corporate and Social Responsibility standards through our actions and our brands'

Figure 3.2

Whether or not you devise a mission statement, the goals for your business should be summarised in the Executive Summary, together with an indication of their relative priorities. Providing this information ensures that the reader can see immediately your business's specific focus.

Rehearsing your Executive Summary

If you are using your plan primarily as a route map for your business, and have no need for outside funding, then there is not very much point in refining and polishing your summary, is there? Wrong. Your plan may indeed be a route-map, and it is possible that your business needs neither outside equity funding nor overdraft facilities from its bank. However, at many points in business life you will need the verbal version of your Executive Summary, your elevator pitch.

Tip

Invest time in your verbal summary, your pitch, work on it until it comes to you easily. Make sure that you can conjure it up at a moment's notice wherever you happen to be, in a crowded train, a taxi or sat in a restaurant.

Opportunity in business very rarely waits patiently for someone to notice it. More often, business opportunities career into view out of what may have seemed like relatively insignificant side turnings, pass by briefly and at speed, before turning to scrabble off again out of sight and out of reach. Your business must be ready to grasp each opportunity very firmly, and only the well-prepared are able to do that.

Make sure that you have rehearsed thoroughly the verbal version of your Executive Summary so that it is available whenever you need it, ready to trip off your tongue. It will let you make a very rapid impression that lets your business seize suitable passing opportunities before they disappear into the distance.

Your polished pitch must be available whether you find yourself sitting next to a potential source of funding, or are finalising a large sales contract with a major new customer, or trying to recruit a critically important employee, someone whose recruitment would make things happen for your business but who is hesitating in the face of uncertainty. Your narrative, those able-to-be-backed-up insights from your plan's Executive Summary, will then serve your business very well indeed.

Conclusion

There is a truism that says that you do not get a second chance to make a first impression, a sentiment that certainly applies to your business plan's Executive Summary. Write it last, write it when you have completed the rest of your plan and are really able to communicate what your business is all about and the features that will ensure its success.

It should summarise your business's market, and highlight the key factors that ensure that your business will be successful in meeting customers' needs. Outline clearly what separates your business from its rivals, giving it a vital competitive edge, and, not least, explain about your own ability to deliver and that of your team.

A well-written Executive Summary will make its readers want to find out more about a business. Respect your readers' time, brevity is essential, but ensure nonetheless that you cover the key areas.

Here is the checklist:

- The reasons that I have prepared this business plan are these, including a clear statement of funding need if appropriate.

- My business's customers are these and their needs are these.
- My business meets those needs better than its rivals because of these factors, which are difficult for others to replicate for the following reasons.
- This is me and my team and these factors about us show you that we can deliver.
- The following statements summarise our goals.

Do not exaggerate, but business is not the place to be reticent. If your business requires outside financial backing or internal corporate funding, remember that professional investors and corporate decision-makers would much rather be impressed by your plan than reject it. Once you contemplate their thought processes, you will realise that they are hungry for credible business opportunities that need financial backing. They have to invest somewhere. Make sure that your plan's Executive Summary summarises exactly why your ideas represent an excellent business proposition. Make them want to find out more.

Finally, in business it is not always possible to predict when the door of opportunity will open a fraction, providing a narrow gap, an entrance into a major business opening. It may arise as a result of a chance meeting, perhaps, at a business breakfast presentation, on a train, or in a café. The opportunity may exist only for a very short time. At such moments, if you can turn the contents of your Executive Summary into an elevator pitch, you may be able to seize that moment before it passes and seize the opportunity before it passes.

That is on occasion how business works, of course, securing opportunities before they disappear, and then making them work. Management theories are very helpful, they provide fresh insights, and they provide business tools and techniques to use. They supply the craft and sometimes even the fine art of business management, but for all of that, straight lines and clear views and predictable cause and effects remain a rarity in the real world.

Successful businesses harness management theory to their advantage, but always remain alert for the unexpected opportunities that will sometimes come past.

INSTANT TIP

By definition the Executive Summary can only be written properly once the rest of your plan is substantially complete.

04

People: how do I show that I (and the people around me) have what it takes?

Let me tell you the secret that has led me to my goal, my strength lies solely in my tenacity.

Louis Pasteur

You need the self-esteem to hire people who are smarter than you and give them the autonomy to manage their own areas. Surround yourself with great people and then get out of the way.

Howard Schulz, Starbucks

Introduction

Throughout human history people have been in business, economic exchange is a norm for mankind. Bartering, the exchange of items of utility and value such as tools and weapons, animal skins and food, items of personal adornment, followed the last very few thousand years by ways of storing that utility and value so that it can be drawn upon later. The thing we call money, of course.

Primary school children's behaviour in the playground indicates how readily human beings engage in barter activities. Even when very young, children easily assign worth to collected items and toys and exchange these with each other for perceived fair value. Being 'in business', negotiating with others in economic deals, is not an alien activity separate from the rest of human existence, it has been fundamental to it for tens of thousands of years.

Entrepreneurial activity is at the heart of 21st-century worldwide economics. It is studied at school, and at graduate and post-graduate degree level. The internet provides immediately available and completely flexible access to opportunities for personal and management skills development, allowing individuals to select learning experiences that fit individual lifestyles. Learning can be more structured and formalised, or informal and ad hoc.

Setting up and then growing any business to achieve sustained success demands a complex mix of innate skills and learned behaviours. That blend contains personal attributes and abilities, which themselves continue to develop over time and with experience, and skills acquired from more formalised training and learning programmes.

Stereotypes

In a training course setting, ten minutes spent brainstorming with a group of managers and a flipchart will produce a version of the following personal attributes that people commonly associate with business success:

Confidence, enthusiasm, conviction

Confidence may be loud, or it can be understated and quiet, but being out there in business means being out there. It means believing in what you are doing and in your ability to do it, and selling yourself and your ideas to potential financial backers, customers, and key employees. Enthusiasm is infectious, and conviction is essential.

Low levels of personal conviction will leak out somewhere to betray you no matter what words you employ, in your tone of voice, in your body language. Others will spot the clues and draw their own conclusions. If it is possible to fool some people all of the time, it will not be very many.

Motivation, hunger for success

If running a business is like driving a vehicle, then motivation is the high-octane fuel. Motivation is formidable in its effects, and powers successful individuals over, through or around obstacles. A person who is truly motivated to do something will almost always do that thing in the end, no matter how long it takes.

Many successful entrepreneurs are driven to succeed, and most seek recognition of their achievements. Even ostentation may contain diverse messages. For some people the cars they drive may indeed say something like 'just look how well I'm doing', but equally it might be a case of '*please* see how well I'm doing', which is rather different.

Risk-taking

Some people are more comfortable working with higher risk levels than others. Being in business is about taking calculated risks, meaning fully considered. Blind leaps of faith are for the very brave and the very foolhardy, and have their place at the roulette table rather than in business.

Determination, tenacity

Business life is often tough and always has set-backs. It is an unforgiving place and you need an ability to dig deep when things fail despite your best efforts, and to persevere when things go wrong, as they will. Sometimes tough decisions are required, and those decisions will make you unpopular. Entrepreneurs must be hard-headed when necessary, which is not the same thing as hard-hearted of course.

Self-reliance, self-determination

An approach to life that says 'I can do this' is an essential attribute, possession of an inner certainty that, no matter what twists and turns you encounter, you will be able to negotiate them successfully. Henry Ford once observed that whether you believe that you can do a thing, or whether you believe that you can't, you are right either way.

What really makes an entrepreneur?

A considerable body of academic research has focused upon this area, namely identifying the skill sets possessed by successful entrepreneurs. Pioneering research into entrepreneurship in the 1970s was led by Jeffrey Timmons and carried out at the

Massachusetts Institute of Technology (MIT). The results allow entrepreneurs to reflect upon their own personal profiles.

The list below incorporates findings from the MIT study, and includes some areas that typical brainstorm session results may omit:

- High levels of drive and energy, and a passion to make things happen.
- High levels of self-belief and self-confidence.
- Being a self-starter, which means high levels of initiative.
- Believing that you are able to influence and change things, that you are in charge of your own destiny.
- An ability to work comfortably with ambiguous information, certainty is not always available in business.
- A low level of fear of failure.
- An ability to take considered risks.
- A willingness to stay around for long-haul to achieve results.
- Seeing the making of money not as an end in itself, but as just one of several valid measures of success.
- Seeking continuous feedback to keep watch on what's actually happening out there.
- Having an ability for 'continuous pragmatic problem solving', an ability to fix things on the hoof.
- Ability to secure the resources needed.
- Relying upon self-imposed internal standards.
- Setting clear goals that need to be achieved.

None of these attributes is an absolute, either possessed by an individual or not. Each is an attribute that an individual might have more or less of a predisposition towards. In any event, observation suggests that these separated behavioural characteristics will actually be related, high levels of self-esteem and confidence might be linked to an individual possessing a low level fear of failure, for example.

> ## Tip
>
> The 'perfect' entrepreneur does not exist, an injection of reality that many find reassuring. Although the personal characteristics that tend to lead to entrepreneurial success can be identified, different recipes, different combinations will be needed for each specific business opportunity depending upon specific individual circumstances. Furthermore, those circumstances themselves are not constant, but change. The business situations that prevail at the outset, internally and externally, will most certainly change and keep on changing as a business grows and develops.

During the start-up stages for a business, the business founder will usually be forced to hold all the strings, to manage everything themselves, very closely, in order to keep all of the plates spinning. As a business grows, the founder has to be able to let go more, start to delegate, to recruit able people to fill specialist roles in marketing, HR, finance, production, systems far better than the founder themselves could.

Another particularly important point is that, since one individual on their own may not possess a high level of the all of the listed characteristics, strengths in some areas can compensate for deficiencies in others. Possessing a fierce determination to succeed can and does carry things a long way in business terms, therefore, even if a person with that attribute in high measure finds it difficult to work with somewhat ambiguous information, for example.

Nature and nurture and attitudes to risk

Many behavioural attributes seem to be shaped by genes, then moulded by personal experience during people's formative years and fine-tuned by the course of their business careers. People's outlook also changes during the different stages of life, and according to the size of their safety net in terms of their private financial position and to the extent of their responsibilities for others' well-being.

In other words, personal attributes do not exist in a vacuum, but are instead affected all the time by the circumstances of people's lives.

Individuals in secure, well-paid jobs who have large mortgages and young children will probably have a lower risk-taking profile than those with fewer responsibilities and less to lose. In fact, nothing much to lose is a pretty strong starting position from which to take some very big risks. That may be part of the reason why so many successful entrepreneurs have business failures behind them. They will certainly have learned useful lessons from their mistakes, but quite frankly more than a few may not have had much left to lose.

A magic ingredient?

Benjamin Franklin stated that he was a strong believer in luck, finding that the harder he worked the more he had of it. Some people are certainly natural possessors of a high level of personal charm, a charisma. They are not invariably the most able, but seem to possess a touch of magic when random events usually appear to break in their direction. Others may indeed perceive them as more lucky in the outcome of chance and non-chance events than themselves.

> ## Tip
>
> Behaving in ways that others perceive as charismatic may reflect certain innate skills, but these may also have been perfected consciously. Certainly a degree of charisma can be acquired through observing and reflecting on the behaviour of charismatic people, and of course many self-development programmes are available.

Quite what a charismatic individual's magnetic presence really comprises will be a very complex question, but where it is present in a business context it will be employed to win over hard-nosed investors, bank managers, customers, and even tax inspectors. I have watched this process happen on a number of occasions when the odds were all stacked in the opposite direction. I have watched how, for example, over the course of two hours, the principal of a multi-franchise car dealership was able to win over not one but two senior inspectors during a tax inspection. I provided all the necessary technical back-up and support, but the decisive factor that made the difference to whether HM Revenue and Customs wound up the case or decided to pursue it was the personal charisma of the business owner. There was certainly no question of fraud in any event, but my client saved himself from enormous costs and stress using charm and wit.

This book has said several times that your business plan is necessarily and essentially about you. Review your own interpersonal skills, and hone them if you wish. If you can develop a management style that works for you, your ability to carry others along with you, engaging their support in helping you to steer your business towards its objectives, will certainly be enhanced.

Of course, you may already be one of the naturally charismatic few, or you may have to work at things a little. Successful entrepreneurs each have their own style, one that works for them, that is moulded around their own personality and the ways in which they interact with others.

Rather less charming and more autocratic managerial styles also succeed in business, of course. Teflon-coated rhinoceros-hide works too, but even the severest autocrats can possess quite a lot of personal charm behind the facade, and will persuade when they cannot cajole.

People skills

Being in business is ultimately about people: customers, employees, colleagues, owners. The business world, a free market, is a brutally honest place when it comes to personal interactions. If you fear rejection, and many people do, it may help if you can anticipate rejection without expecting it. It will certainly help in the long run if you can acquire a tough skin, business is business, things are not always personal.

Work hard on the people skills that work for you, and try to find ways of working successfully with the widest variety of others. Whatever your own approach is, if it does not work, if you are not able either to win over the people that you need to, then your business will have a major handicap. Those people are not just its customers, but key employees, bankers and potential funders.

Tip

Many entrepreneurs demonstrate management styles that seem to sit easily with their underlying personalities, providing a seamless front. Logic would suggest that if the people they interact with know that they are dealing with the real thing, then the communication process will be a lot more direct and quite possibly more effective.

Personality profiles

This section of your business plan will include your CV, but it would be unusual for it to include also a personality profile. The behavioural side of things does not feature very prominently in business planning guides, but understanding yourself and what makes you tick will help your business planning endeavours considerably.

As humans we are each unique, we possess different blends of personal skills and attributes, determined by our genes and shaped by our backgrounds, environment and experiences, as noted above. Some people prefer precision and detail, and are comfortable with a step-by-step sequential approach to planning, often driven from the top downwards. At the other end of the spectrum are more spontaneous types, individuals who dislike straight lines and boundaries. Their preference is for as much flexibility as possible.

In the real world there exist many successful entrepreneurs who are not naturally attracted by the idea of formalised planning. Yet those same individuals, when asked, can invariably explain the big business development plan to which they are working. Their scripts may not always be committed to writing, which puts them at a disadvantage in many respects, but the big underlying plan is in place.

There are numerous ways in which things can go wrong in business terms, but only a very limited number of ways in which they can go right. I have never met a successful entrepreneur who said 'I don't have a clue where this business is going', since people with that type of mindset will fail. The only questions would be which aspect of their business activities would go wrong badly enough to sink the business, and how large a cushion of resources exists to delay that end.

As with the cliché about verbal contracts, undocumented plans may not be worth the paper they are not written on. It is certainly true that if funding or other resources need to be secured from others, then a written plan is essential. It is also true that only written plans set out readily measurable targets, and set unambiguous deadlines and delegated responsibilities. Without a hugely focused and controlling entrepreneur at the helm, informal plans carried only in the head may simply be evidenced by ever-moving goalposts that employees find very difficult to cope with.

On the other hand, born planners risk their business ambitions never emerging from the earliest stages, from a fearful fog of too much uncertainty. People who value a high degree of precision and accuracy, for whom spontaneity feels threatening, may sometimes do anything rather than actually do anything. No action equals no business.

Tip

You will know whether you are a natural planner or not, so try to cultivate a sense of proportion. Aim for balance, walking a line between too much planning and too little. Spontaneous knee-jerk responses to every potential threat on the horizon are as damaging to any business's prospects of success as a safety-first approach of planning everything with so much detail and rigidity that a straitjacket is created and nothing at all can change, or even start.

Strength from different perspectives

An individual who possesses a substantial measure of entrepreneurial attributes, and no large negatives that cancel the positives out (a penchant for law-breaking, for example), has what it takes to succeed in business. He or she will succeed more easily, however, when they understand that their world-view is only one perspective, and that others will have different ways of seeing and doing things. Anyone who sees the views of others as threatening is simply demonstrating their own lack of self-confidence.

> ## Tip
> Your ability to perceive business issues from a number of different perspectives increases the number of options you have available for handling them. If you ask yourself 'how does my customer/supplier/employee see this issue?' you will find that new pathways for solving problems immediately open up.

We have come back to the grizzly bear on the trail. If you and your team can marshal the attributes and resources needed to outrun your competitors, your travelling companions on the business journey, then you have maximised your chances of surviving. Furthermore, seeing the business trail as a distance race rather than a sprint will enable you to appreciate the bear story as a metaphor for the whole life of a business, not just for the immediate and most pressing problem.

Relying on a single attribute, speed, for example, will not be sufficient in itself, however, if your fellow hikers have other attributes that cancel yours out – more acute hearing perhaps, or a better sense of smell, and therefore possess the ability to identify the bear's presence before you do. To prevent them obtaining a head start that could prove fatal to your business, your job as manager is to ensure that it has access to whatever resources it requires, whatever provides it with metaphorical binoculars to scan a more distant horizon, and whatever comprises the best metaphorical footwear for the terrain over which it chooses to travel.

Over time you will change the equipment that your business needs, and your companions on the trail will be doing the same; you may have to recruit specialist members of your team and provide them with metaphorical binoculars that have night vision, in order to stay just that vital fraction ahead of the competition. The name of the game lies in finding and using small marginal advantages that let your business stay further ahead of the bear than your rivals can.

Know yourself

Over many years' experience of running business courses, the most fascinating area for many participants has been undertaking what are known as psychometric tests, in order to better understand themselves as managers. Test results are always seized upon eagerly, and subsequent feedback and discussion sessions to review the results and their implications are very lively. Exercises that sometimes people were slightly wary of at first become highlights, and often bring the enlightenment that comes from self-understanding. There are frequent 'Eureka!' moments.

Two categories of psychometric tests exist. The first type assesses mental agility, such as a person's verbal and non-verbal reasoning skills, and their level of numeracy. They provide indications of a person's overall mental ability and are collectively known as cognitive tests. Cognitive tests are often used in selection processes for jobs, and, putting things rather crudely, measure brainpower.

The second type consists of assessments of personality type, what makes a person tick and how they see the world. Psychometric profiling exercises of the second type allow individuals to understand better their own psychological make-up, and that of the people they work with. By learning more about yourself, you can gain understanding about the types of business situations and tasks that you will naturally be able to handle well, and those in which you are likely to perform less well.

Those insights can confer huge advantages when running a business. Everyone has areas where they are less strong, and understanding where your weaknesses lie lets you can take conscious steps to compensate for them. Conversely, as long as you remain unaware of them your blind spots can put you at a disadvantage.

A variety of very well-respected psychometric test exercises exists; they usually take the form of questionnaires and used to analyse an individual's behavioural areas that have implications for business life. These behavioural areas include basic personality types, attitudes to life and likely responses to different situations. The cognitive tests examine ability levels, both general and specific job-related abilities. The purpose of all these tests is for individuals to be able to understand more of what makes them uniquely themselves, and to understand the implications of that knowledge for their business activities.

The importance of a team approach

Driving a business forward requires various types of management skills. Harder, analytical ones that are needed to remain diligent in scanning the business horizon, and softer, more creative ones that provide the flexibility to identify novel and pragmatic solutions to business problems. The existence of a team can provide that range of approaches. Your own team may comprise fellow employees, of course, or outside contacts and advisers, or probably a mixture of both.

Team structures matter, since no one individual possesses a full range of business and interpersonal skills on their own. When you have made yourself aware of your own gaps then you can go about the process of finding competent and complementary individuals to fill them. When looking at other successful businesses from the outside, particularly larger ones, the breadth and depth of team abilities available may be obscured by the presence of larger-than-life and charismatic figureheads. The range of underlying abilities will nevertheless be there in full support. Note the inclusion in Figure 3.2 of Cadbury Schweppes plc's goal to 'deepen talent pool'.

Depending upon your business's needs and each specific situation, people can be brought in on an as-needed basis, or employed full time or part time. In the real world there are experienced outsiders who are appointed frequently to take a 'non-executive' director role. That means that they are company directors and therefore legally responsible for the company's affairs and actions, but do not work full time in the business.

Businesses need to recruit able, loyal, and motivated key team members to achieve success, and a good business plan addresses those issues. As a fundamental part of that, getting the reward and remuneration structures and incentives right is a fine balancing act, and this area will need careful thought also. The essentials must be spelled out in your plan, the following questions will help to trigger your thoughts:

- How will key team members share in the future success of your business and thus be motivated to help ensure that success?
- How will their services be retained for as long as it takes to succeed?
- What safeguards are there for your business if they leave?
- Do they see a direct link between their individual contributions and what the business gives back to them, both now and into the future?
- How will their job performance, their contribution to the business, be measured?
- Should they own a slice of the business? Would the potential future benefits from such ownership help to compensate them for what may be a lower personal income level in the short term than they have previously enjoyed, or might achieve elsewhere for their skills?

Your team is larger than you think

In terms of team, many business plans limit themselves to company directors and other key employees. Your business connections are also a fundamental part of your team, your contacts really matter. The people who are able to contribute to your business's success comprise in fact a much wider group than just key employees.

The following list highlights potential members of your wider team. Your business plan should indicate the people in these sorts of roles who will add something significant to the likelihood of business success:

- Your business's bank manager, accountant, solicitor.
- Someone else with the skills and experience to act as mentor and sounding board.
- Satisfied customers acting as word-of-mouth selling agents.
- Other business owners, not necessarily in same industry, particularly if they are at a similar stage of business growth.

To ensure that you can appreciate the full potential membership of your wider team, using a spider-diagram approach here works well. Draw bubbles or boxes for each business connection that you have, and then see where your thoughts then lead you. You will discover that you possess many more potentially useful contacts than you at first imagine.

Use the list above to begin, then add others, such as classmates from school and college who might be helpful, potentially useful people that you have met socially or at business networking events, members of your circle of friends and relatives. Being out and about in as many ways as possible always increases the number of your connections.

> **Tip**
>
> Find ways of maximising your exposure to potentially useful people. That may sound uncomfortably pushy, or perfectly acceptable, depending upon your own personality and attitudes. Being in business will force you, time after time, outside of the boundaries of your own personal comfort zone, wherever those happen to lie.

If you feel uncomfortable on occasion that is normal, it means that you are forcing yourself outside of your own 'safe' boundaries as you progress into more foreign territory that you need to penetrate.

Sales skills

On the subject of being uncomfortable, selling is a word that some find faintly distasteful, and it is mentioned here specifically for that reason. Being in business means, as a minimum, that you are very often selling yourself, whether or not you also hold a formal sales remit. Sales skills and techniques can be learned, although some individuals are naturally more able to sell whereas others find it somewhat harder.

> **Tip**
>
> If you happen to be in the majority, the second group, consider the following. Once you have analysed, really analysed, your customers' needs, and once you have then fine-tuned your product or service to meet those clearly defined needs, you will find that your confidence to sell will soar. The reason is that once you yourself are convinced that your business has a winning formula, something that will bring real, tangible, explainable benefits to your desired customers, then you will find it easy to persuade others.

Born salesperson or not, once you are convinced of the benefits that your business provides, then you will be able to sell those benefits. The words you use, the tone of your voice, your body language, all will back you up. And people will believe you.

Need for financial commitment

The chapter on business finances comes later, but there is an important issue that links into the people section of your business plan.

Where a business plan seeks to obtain financial backing, would-be funders expect to see clear indicators of commitment from the key individual(s). That commitment can be demonstrated by personal investment in the business, and by ensuring, for example, that an element of management's remuneration packages is linked directly to the achievement of desired, measurable, business goals.

Potential backers are not willing to risk substantial slices of future profits being extracted from a business by means of management salaries and bonuses. When outside funds are being invested, tightly drawn legal contracts are normally put into place at the outset in order to govern the power of senior management in this area.

As another condition precedent for outside investment, potential funders will also seek to ensure that ownership remains tightly controlled. Contracts will be put into place for example to ensure that if a shareholding employee were to leave the business for what had been pre-designated as the 'wrong' reasons, leaving to join a competitor perhaps, then all shares held by that person would have to be returned under pre-set buy-back terms.

The legal aspects of equity funding deals are complex, be aware that you will always need to take legal advice from a solicitor with specialist knowledge.

Conclusion

Your own role is pivotal to the success of your business, and anyone who is asked to back your business is essentially being asked to back you and any team that surrounds you. Your business plan will, consciously or subconsciously, reveal to readers the aspects of you that will make the business succeed. Or not.

No one is perfect, but consistently successful entrepreneur would be able to tick 'yes' to most of the statements below. The important word there is 'most':

- I am determined to make my business succeed.
- I control my own destiny.
- I am not easily discouraged.
- I observe and learn from others.
- I always get something out of situations that go wrong.
- I want recognition for my achievements.
- I am not motivated by money alone.
- I will sacrifice work-life balance to work long hours when needed.
- I am able to take calculated risks.
- I can switch off and refresh my batteries when needed.
- I see the big picture but also focus on fine details.
- I am good at ideas but I also finish things once I have started them.

No one individual possesses all of the skills needed to set up and then grow a business, and you should remember the importance of having, and drawing upon the skills of, the wider business team around you. Fortunately, that team will be larger than you at first imagine.

In the final analysis, all business financial performance is driven by people, by their will and their expertise. No individual can possess all of the business skills needed, and the wider team brings an essential diversity to any business. That diversity is about the skills available, but also about personality traits and outlook on life. Your business plan needs to show that a balance of skills is in place.

Just as you must seek to achieve constant improvements in your business, you can build your business experience and skills using methods that best suit your situation. Certainly, maximise your exposure to other businesspeople, observe for yourself what works for them and what doesn't, and aim to understand why.

Selling skills will come naturally when you believe that your business offering meets customer needs very well indeed. Get your business plan right, particularly get your customer focus, and you will probably find that you become an able and persuasive salesperson.

At that point called sales, people issues merge into marketing issues. If you keep very closely focused on your chosen customers, find out exactly what their needs are and fit your offering to match those needs, then you will discover that the sales and marketing parts of your business plan start to fall into place.

INSTANT TIP

No one individual possesses all of the business skills needed and a wider team brings an essential diversity to any business. Your business plan needs to show that a balance of skills is in place.

05

The business: how do I explain what makes this so special?

Never invest in a business that you cannot understand.
Warren Buffet

Introduction

Business plan authors are normally very familiar with the detail of their businesses, something is clearly wrong if they are not. Many people find therefore this inward-looking part of a business plan is the easiest to write. That does not mean that it is easy to write well.

This section of the plan provides the platform for explaining all about your business. It should describe your business concept and its stage of market readiness, and if appropriate identify further stages that must be completed and their expected timescale.

In overview, this section of your business plan will contain these three connected elements:

- A detailed explanation of your business's product or service.
- An outline of the operations, how things will work.
- A pervading theme of how your business's offering meets customers' needs.

> ## Tip
>
> When drafting this section of your plan, the emphasis to bear firmly in mind is that of demonstrating the features of your business in the context of how they are different from rivals. As you explain your business, demonstrate what gives your business an edge, its competitive advantage.

The buzzword is Unique Selling Proposition (USP). This highlights what features of a business's offering meet customers' needs better, and why rivals find those special features difficult to replicate.

It is your customers' views that matter, their perceptions of your product or service, not yours. That is why USP has more recently acquired a younger sibling, the UPB or Unique Perceived Benefit. The UPB's focus is that of the buyer, their perspective, their perception of the potential benefits that are obtainable.

An objective view

You believe in your business, you need to be positive, but you must to keep both the tone and content objective, essential if funding is required. Any claims that you make must be supported by evidence, and that evidence must be able to stand up to unbiased scrutiny.

Tip

To reduce the risk of your enthusiasm carrying your thoughts away, it can be particularly helpful for this section of the plan to recruit someone suitably objective and possessing the right experience to act as a devil's advocate and sounding board. Simply by being 'not you', they will be able to provide new perspectives and fresh insights.

Another potential benefit is that as you recruit someone to perform that role you can take the opportunity to rehearse elements of your elevator pitch. As the chapter on your plan's Executive Summary explains, that pitch is a potent weapon in your business armoury in many different situations.

In the previous chapter, benefits arising from a team approach to business were identified. The sounding board role should be distinct from that team, more objective, more of a business mentor. Finding a competent individual to act in that role can also become a long-term investment for your business, since the right person can remain on tap as your business grows.

To find the right person, you need to establish carefully whose views you trust, and why. Your own business technical background and your own personality type, can help you to determine the type of person that you are looking for. If you have undertaken any of the psychometric tests outlined in the previous chapter, the results will be helpful to you now. Aim for someone whose technical strengths are in areas that are not your technical strengths, and whose personality type is not your personality type.

The more common possibilities are these:

- Individuals who have operated at senior level within large business. Such people can be a good source of business wisdom, as long as they really do understand the differences that pervade smaller, possibly more flexible business cultures, where there are generally fewer fixed rules and fewer layers, and where getting something done can happen very quickly.

- Successful entrepreneurs can make very good sounding boards. Experience matters though, breadth of vision, and individuals who have run businesses for relatively short periods may have depth in terms of their own sector, but not breadth. If someone has built up and then sold a business, that is a plus, but beware anyone who believes that they know everything. No one possesses a monopoly of business wisdom, nobody is infallible.

- Professional business advisers bring much objectivity. Good ones will have encountered many businesses during their careers. Running any business is not about the rigid application of set rules, however, so make sure that any accountants and solicitors on your list possess demonstrable creative thinking skills to match their analytical ones. Bank managers can possess valuable insights and will certainly have seen many businesses, but some may be rather risk averse.

Tip

The person that you are looking for exists somewhere within your network of contacts, and their contacts. Search thoroughly and you will find them. Related to that, and so often the case in business life, the process of doing something, well, can generate other quite unexpected benefits as a by-product. The search for someone to act as mentor may well turn up other useful alliances and opportunities.

Never doubt the sheer power of getting on with things in business, even the ones that appear to be the most daunting.

How to explain about your business

In terms of writing about your product or service in detail, pitch your explanations at the level of a reasonably intelligent non-specialist in your industry, and always avoid using jargon. Jargon alienates people, makes them feel like outsiders, and you do not want to risk losing your hard-won readership.

Describe the structure of your business, actual or proposed. Outline its history and background, but do not expend too much effort in explaining the past, just enough to provide readers with context. Your business is about the future of course and, safer and much more certain place that the past may be, your business plan's task is to explain your business's future.

When writing about the business, readers will want to know that you have a firm focus on what factors drive profits in your sector. The stream of potential profits available from your product or service depends upon two factors. The first is how much profit is available in the sector in which your business operates, the second is how much power your business has in order to take as much of the available profit as possible.

Unless your business has a monopoly of supply, created by patent protection of ideas perhaps, or is in a near-monopolistic situation, profits will be earned by creating more value in customers' eyes than rivals' offerings do. That means creating enough value in their opinion that they will pay sufficient sums for your product or service to make it worthwhile that you stay in business.

This is right-wing economics, of course. That business ethos being that as much of the profit potentially available to all businesses in an industry should be taken by the strongest. Unless you are powerful enough to be able to distort the workings of the free market, the bottom line is that dominance can be achieved only by ensuring that your product or service meets customers' perceived needs better than anyone else's.

Operations

This section of your business plan must address how the operational side of things will be structured.

> **Tip**
> There is a fine line to tread here. Do not overload your business plan with operational details, but include all key points. Your aim is to demonstrate how the operational side of things will run efficiently, which includes the methods by which the operational processes will be kept under frequent review in order to keep fine-tuning them.

For smaller businesses, where there just one senior manager is involved or perhaps a few, the successful ones tend to be run by people who possess a strategic view and can see the big picture, but are still able focus upon the detail of operational processes. Management skills of two different orders are required. The first is an ability to handle the big strategic issues, the second a willingness to assimilate fine detail. Successful operations management means having enough detailed focus to keep things firmly on track.

Some individuals span these extremes, but more tend to be more comfortable with the big picture, or with the detail. A major advantage of any team structure is that it comprises different individuals, each bringing different skills and perspectives. Some will be better at strategy, some at operational delivery. We have arrived right back at the place called 'know yourself', of course.

For your business plan, the following list of operational issues will get your thought process started:

- What are the premises requirements for production, storage space, and office space? Consider size, location, future expansion issues, period of lease commitment.

- What general and specialised plant and equipment is needed? Is it better to purchase or lease? For specialised equipment, is it readily available?
- Should any operational areas be outsourced, and why? Areas for potential outsourcing go right across the board, and include logistics and transport, storage, finance, IT, human resources, health and safety, sub-contract manufacturing, self-employed sales agents.
- What legislative and regulatory regime applies to your specific products or services? What is the impact of such regulations?
- How will supplies of vital inputs be secured? These might include the recruitment of a labour force with the necessary specialist skills or knowledge, or an unskilled one that you are able to train, and also the lines of supply for any scarce raw materials required.
- Should the whole business be undertaken by someone else under some form of licensing or franchise arrangement? How would it work? What controls and protections would be needed to protect your business?

The Five Forces model

During the 1970s, Professor Michael Porter developed the Five Forces business model. This very well-known and much-used model can provide many insights about the competitive forces that drive profit levels in your industry, and it can be used to relate those forces to specific businesses. The model looks at the relative strengths of the forces in the industry, thus determining the amount of profit available to all players, all businesses competing for a slice of the cake.

The five forces can be summarised as follows:

- **Degree of competition**: the lower the competitive rivalry between businesses in an industry, the higher the profits. The greater the competition, the lower the profits.

- **Threat of new entrants**: the more difficult it is for newcomers to enter an industry to take a share of the profits available, the higher the profits.
- **Threat of substitutes**: the fewer the number of other products or services that meet equivalent buyer needs, the higher the profits.
- **Buyer bargaining power**: the lower the control that sellers have, the lower the profits. Strong buyers force prices down by driving ever harder bargains with sellers.
- **Supplier bargaining power**: the more power that suppliers have, the lower the profits. Suppliers can take more of the available profits if they control resources needed by the sellers, including raw materials, skilled labour force, specialised production facilities, access to intellectual property rights such as patents.

Porter's Five Forces model can be used to analyse any industry, and reveal whether a business operates within a fundamentally high profit environment or not. Use the questions below as triggers to let you carry out the analysis for your business.

- **Degree of competition**
    - How many sellers are there, few or many?
    - Do a small number of sellers control the industry?
    - If your business does face few competitors, why are there not more?
    - Is competition largely based on selling price?
    - Are your business's products or services basic commodities, difficult to differentiate from rivals' offerings, or are they more complex in nature?
    - Where an established market leader exists, how would it react to the threat posed by new entrants? Does it possess the will, and the financial strength, to attack

new rivals?
- Does surplus production capacity exist?
- **Threat of new entrants**
  - Will other entrants to your business's industry emerge?
  - Can your business's offering be easily replicated?
  - What specific entry barriers exist? Factors such as high capital investment needed, technical know how, regulatory controls, access to specialised technology.
  - Are there economies of scale available to existing players that make new entrants' cost levels uncompetitive?
- **Existence of substitutes**
  - What substitute products or services exist?
  - How close are they? What differences do buyers perceive?
  - How readily are buyers persuaded to switch to substitutes?
- **Extent of buyer bargaining power**
  - How many buyers are there, few or many?
  - Is buyer demand growing, level, or in decline?
  - Are buyers locked into long-term contracts?
  - Are buyers influenced by fashions and trends?
  - Is demand subject to cyclical variations?
  - Are buyers loyal or fickle?
  - Is it easy and inexpensive for buyers to change suppliers?
  - Are buyers used to switching suppliers?
- **Extent of supplier bargaining power**
  - Are there many suppliers, or few?
  - Do they have many customers, or few?
  - Do potential shortages of inputs exist?
  - Are there potential bottlenecks in your business's chain of supply?
  - Do suppliers control input prices?

Porter's model allows you to consider the relative intensity of each force, and gain a clear indication of the likely overall level of available profits. An extreme situation can be used to make the point clearly.

Profits will be low in industry situations where:

- The competition is able and aggressive.
- Barriers to entry are low and therefore new entrants can readily enter the market to obtain a slice of the action.
- A range of close substitute products or services exists.
- Buyers possess high levels of power and can exert control.
- Suppliers possess high levels of power and can exert control.

Such an industry would be a fundamentally low profit one. Match manual car-washing businesses to the above profile and you will see the profit profile.

Reverse all of the above factors, however, and a very high profit business becomes visible. An ideal business operates with little competition, high entry barriers around it, few ready substitutes, many small buyers who need the product or service, and readily available supplies of all necessary inputs. You have heard of Microsoft?

What about the influence of the management team?

No matter how brilliant an entrepreneur and manager you happen to be, the truth is that if your business operates in a fundamentally unattractive industry, it is probably doomed to failure in any event.

Management skill and experience really matters, capable and determined managers will always out-perform poor ones.

However, and as elegantly observed by Warren Buffet: 'When a management team with a reputation for brilliance tackles a business with a reputation for bad economics, it is the reputation of the business that remains intact.' There exists also an older and far less refined piece of wisdom, the one about silk purses and sows' ears.

The good news for less able management is that the reverse holds true also. At the extreme, in industries where demand is soaring, where there are no close substitutes, where competition levels are weak, where high entry barriers exist, where input costs are low for raw materials and labour, and supplies readily available, a relatively unskilled management team will almost certainly develop a profitable business. That business may not be as profitable as it might have been, but it will be profitable nonetheless.

If you believe that someone of little inherent ability has built a successful long-term business, then you have misjudged that person badly, or you will find that their business operates in an environment that largely matches the above description.

All forces are not created equal

In the real world it will often be just one or two of the forces that determine profit levels in an industry, such as the existence of very high entry barriers, or perhaps the monopoly or near monopoly conditions created by the existence of patent protection. For your business plan, determine which forces are dominatingly influential, and consider their implications carefully. Those thoughts and conclusions will be needed later to back up your business plan's statements about your business's profit potential.

> **Tip**
>
> Be frank with yourself. Do not allow your personal belief in a business to distort your perception of the five forces. If your analysis suggests that your business may be operating after all in an industry that gives little chance for sustained profit performance, and where nothing that you can do can retrieve that situation very much, it is far better to find that out at the business planning stage. The alternative will be to discover the same thing later, and the hard way.

If, on the other hand, your analysis makes you ever more convinced that excellent opportunities for profit exist in your chosen industry, then take your analysis a stage further. What can you do to secure your business's position? What barriers to entry, for example, might be erected rapidly? What can be done to secure adequate supplies of all essential inputs? These are vital points for your business plan. As you use the framework supplied by Porter's model to comprehend your business's situation, so will you be able to identify steps that it must take to reinforce its position.

Change means profit opportunity

The Five Forces model analyses the business forces that exist in the real world. Also in the real world change is a factor. Industries themselves are, of course, dynamic – all change over time, and, as a result, the size and impact of each the five forces will change.

Those changes may result in new opportunities for profit, where they emerge as movements in the relative strengths of the five forces. Thus businesses in the financial services industry reap the additional profits available in that industry as ever-tighter regulation results in higher entry barriers for potential new entrants. Consumer protection at one level reduces the degree of competition on another.

Product life-cycle

The level of market demand for products and services also changes, in what is often referred to as a life-cycle pattern:

- Introduction.
- Growth.
- Maturity.
- Decline.

This theory was first developed by Theodore Levitt and first published in the *Harvard Business Review* during the mid-1960s. For any product or service, the stage reached in its life-cycle will have a direct bearing upon profitability, although the life-cycle concept does not help managers to determine when a given stage will end and the next one begin.

Life-cycle and profitability

The pioneer customers who purchase during the start-up and early growth stages of a new service or product are referred to as early adopters or visionaries. They tend to focus upon intrinsic features of the product or service, the unique benefits that it provides to them. The price that they pay may not be as important to them as performance or image, and they will be willing to pay a premium to secure that.

At that stage innovations will be occurring rapidly in the new product or service, and in whatever marketing activities that surround it. Then, as growth in demand really starts to accelerate and take off, so the higher profit levels available will entice new entrants into the marketplace, direct rivals and the me-too merchants, copycats, and substitutes.

Businesses then place much effort into distinguishing their offerings from those of competitors, so that differentiated products and services appear, as branding and other differentiators become clearly visible. Forces of supply and demand will have their effect upon costs, which may start to increase as the most easily available supplies of raw materials and/or labour are used up and shortages start to appear.

Demand itself begins to flatten out as the industry matures. The focus of competitive effort between businesses moves from the winning of new buyers to poaching them from rivals. Poaching from the competition is the only method for business growth in mature markets, since few new customers remain to be won. During the maturity stage, customers become more price-sensitive, not least because the product or service itself will have become more of a commodity. The focus of competition in a maturing market will move towards price levels rather than emphasising intrinsic features.

Decline always happens in the end, demand having been saturated. Most people now own the product or have access to the service. Other than replacement purchases, there will be very little new demand. In any event technological changes and other innovative developments in product or in service delivery will mean that newer, better, faster, cheaper direct rival or substitute products have emerged to accelerate the decline.

Businesses have to focus inwards during decline, and processes and business efficiency become ever more important. Businesses aim to wring out additional profit drop by drop as they streamline manufacturing and delivery processes. In classic economics terms, the least efficient, and therefore least profitable, businesses are the first to fall by the wayside as businesses fail financially during the decline stage.

However, a twist at the tail end of the life-cycle can occur where circumstances make it difficult for businesses to leave an industry. These are so-called exit-barriers, the ultimate irony for a failing business.

For example, where companies in declining industries are tied into long-term finance agreements for expensive capital equipment, and particularly in situations where the company's directors have provided personal financial guarantees as back-up security for the bank. Those directors may try to keep things going in the hope that something will turn up, rather than wind up the business and get out while there are still some assets left.

For such businesses the decline can become a long, slow process. Individual businesses struggle on, profits falling, and the decline eventually results in sales levels that are too low to achieve break-even, and losses appear. Ultimately, destructive price wars may break out as over-capacity means that the available supply far exceeds demand. The limping survivors in the industry continue to slug it out to hold onto a dwindling level of business from the few remaining customers. In modern Western economies, the lingering survivors may be able to continue for a long time even when the underlying business is a failure. That is because they have increasing freehold values in their balance sheets to support their ever-increasing borrowings.

First mover advantage

In emerging industries, being there early can provide what is called first mover advantage, being ahead of the competition in picking the low-hanging fruit, the easy profits. However, the second wave of entrants to an industry do have the opportunity to analyse how they might themselves do things faster/better/cheaper, and those later, sharper arrivals may be able to exploit that opportunity.

Significant market share captured early on provides a buffer which will protect early entrants, but unless the market leader continues to innovate successfully, to maintain the competitive gap, new entrants will emerge to develop the concept.

Pregnant with profit

People who see many business plans, newly written ones and ones that have done the rounds, are witnesses to a kind of magnet effect when an industry is generally perceived as being pregnant with profit opportunity. Numbers of business plans multiply as more and more potential entrants emerge, attracted by the high growth-stage profits that are available.

When you consider potential profit levels in your industry, ask yourself whether you are looking at an opportunity that looks so attractive from the outside that, if the barriers to entry are low and if differentiators are difficult to find, a throng of new entrants will appear rapidly to erode your business's lead and your profits.

Many of these rivals may not get things quite right and quickly fall by the wayside, but some might start meeting buyers' needs better than your business is able to. Simple Darwinian evolution, really.

There also exist businesses out there operating in industry sectors that are low profile, almost unnoticed. Such businesses can be profitable because they are largely overlooked. The main barrier to entry may simply be invisibility. They are off the radar.

At the unglamorous end of things some types of scrapyard and recycling businesses fit this model, as do road accident clean-up businesses, for example. Conversely, at the more glamorous end of things, but seeking to remain as invisible and discreet as they can, some businesses cater for the ordinary needs of the rich and famous and their discretion not only earns them high profit levels, it also helps to ensure their continued invisibility. Providing paper-shredding services to celebrities may not sound much, but can be very profitable.

Conclusion

Writing about your business requires objectivity; do not allow your enthusiasm to tint your spectacles with a shade of pink.

Porter's Five Forces model provides a framework for analysing the forces that affect the amount of profit available in your industry. It can also indicate in what parts of the industry the larger slices of profit will be earned, and what forces will determine that, vitally important information for your business plan. The product life-cycle concept is also useful, and provides insights about the way that available profit levels will change with time.

Each business is unique, however, every industry is different, and the real world is never as perfect as the theory. Everything is dynamic, and changes with the passage of time.

Out in the real world, your rivals may or may not be using sophisticated business models to try to beat your business. They may not have encountered them even, and if they have they may not be using them to gain insights in a structured way. Your competitors are themselves human, and humans behave in the ways in which they behave. They will certainly try to move in on your patch if they see big profits being earned. Your job, therefore, is to keep innovating, keep your business meeting its customers' needs better than they can, keep differentiating your business's offering, and keep the barriers to entry as high as possible.

For your business plan, and in order to run your business, when you can see and control what is happening better than the competition does, you can make the right decisions to stack more of the odds in your business's favour.

INSTANT TIP

To reduce the risk of your enthusiasm carrying your thoughts away, it can be particularly helpful for the business section of your plan to recruit someone suitably objective to act as devil's advocate.

06

Markets, marketing and the fine art of pricing: how do I show that we really understand what our customers want?

I keep six honest serving-men
(They taught me all I knew);
Their names are What and Why and When
And How and Where and Who

Rudyard Kipling

In the factory we make cosmetics, but in the store we sell hope.

Charles Revson, founder of Revlon

Introduction

Beyond everything, a business must have customers, for without them there is no business. Your business plan must explain about your business's marketplace, its potential buyers. This section requires careful consideration to write well, and unfortunately it is rather easy to produce the marketing section badly.

Weak business plans often turn back inwards at this point, explaining again about the product or service. In addition, the fact that you are convinced by the special features of your business's offering may lead you rather too readily to believe that many buyers will feel the same. As a result, imaginary customers populate the pages of many business plans. The easiest place to locate eager customers is inside the heads of the authors.

The following areas are the ones to focus upon; some you will already have contemplated when you wrote about your business, or rather when you wrote about your business from its customers' perspective:

- Who are your chosen customers?
- Who actually makes the purchase decision?
- Why do they choose to purchase your business's offering? (How does your offering improve buyers' lives in ways that rivals' offerings do not?)
- Into what different segments or niches do buyer groups fall?
- What different needs and buying habits characterise those different groups?
- How will your business gain access to each niche, how will your business's product or service be visible?
- What conclusions arise when you rank your customer groups by relative profit potential?

- How is it as easy as possible for customers to make a purchase?
- What are the perceived benefits to buyers, tangible and intangible?
- What is the overall size of your business's market?
- How is that changing?
- How easy is it to win repeat business?
- How will your offering be priced? And what is the logic for that?

When you have completed the marketing elements of your business plan, by reaching a detailed understanding of customers' needs, then you will have written the most difficult part of your business plan. Addressing the questions above at a superficial level is not difficult, but answering them convincingly certainly is.

Your business plan will be much stronger in this area if your business is already trading, and can demonstrate real sales to real customers. Contracted orders from future customers come a close second. However, start-up business plans commonly confuse the latter with expressions of potential interest:

'I was interested to learn that your company is developing a new digital body blood-flow monitor for post-operative patient monitoring. As the UK's leading healthcare group we are always very keen to learn about new products under development and can confirm that we presently purchase about 150,000 blood-flow related products per year.'

At first reading that wording appears much more substantial than it really is. Would-be buyers express interest about many things, they need to keep tabs on what is available out there. Expressions of interest are not firm orders, much less actual sales.

Market research

Reliable market research is a formidable weapon. Strong business plans use it to provide evidence of buyers' needs, and to confirm how those needs have been objectively established. Market research lets businesses test out ideas on the people that really matter. The feedback obtained allows adjustments to be made to the business offering, and a framework for marketing activities to be designed.

Market research techniques are designed to collect and then analyse data that will provide information about the following questions:

1. What are buyers' needs in the areas concerned, real ones and perceived ones?

2. What does your business's offering look like from the buyer's perspective?

Research can involve directly obtaining the views of selected target groups, by talking to them, and by using surveys and questionnaires. It may also involve the use of published data and statistics, available from business libraries and from the internet. Since your correct business focus is on buyer needs, then the more accurate the focus, the more closely you can match your business's offering to them. Strong business plans back up their assertions about customers with credible and objective research. Always quote your sources, and be especially careful to double-check any data that you obtain from the internet.

The art and the science of pricing

As a marketing tool, prices are easy to understand and relatively easy to change. To maximise the profits generated by your business, your objective is to set prices at the maximum levels that customers are willing to pay for the benefits they obtain from the product or service.

Pricing has roots in the accounting numbers, but is in reality much more a function of customers' perceptions of a number of factors, including brand image, quality, and value for money. Note that we are referring to perceptions again, not to objective reality.

Pricing decisions nearly always contain an element of subjective judgement; they will always be more than just a function of a business's cost structure. It follows that pricing issues sit firmly within the marketing section of your business plan. They do require some financial input, as we will see, but ultimately the pricing of a product or service relies on judgement, not science. That said, possessing a clear understanding of your business's cost structure is essential, and certainly allows better-informed pricing decisions to be made.

Since price levels can be changed easily, when used as a marketing tool they can have a rapid effect upon sales volumes. Set prices too high and your business will lose customers or fail to win them; set them too low and you will not maximise profits.

Tip

Simply talk to your existing and prospective customers, make it interesting for them, how do they perceive price levels in your industry? How do they see your pricing structure as fitting in? Those views are not difficult to obtain and will let you fine-tune prices with much greater confidence.

Know what your customer is actually buying

The Revlon quote at the start of this chapter says much. What factors underpin your customers' buying decisions, what are they really trying to obtain from the purchase? When a person buys a designer suit, how do image considerations weigh against functionality as a garment?

Buyers often display economically irrational decision processes in situations where price levels are used as indicators of quality. The pricing of vanity products such as perfume, jewellery, and some clothing often falls into this category, price and branding joining to create a certain image. Luxury goods generally rely on price messages, as do luxury services, including top hotels and restaurants. The much-used adjective 'exclusive' is loaded with meaning, of course, when you think about it. Items such as works of art, expensive clothing, and motor cars are often priced in ways that have been extremely carefully designed to give important image messages.

Buyers may not need those messages themselves, of course – it may already have occurred to them that they possess rather large bank balances (or borrowings) – but some people's needs include ensuring that others receive that message. It is also true that some people behave in the opposite way – quite the opposite, in fact – preferring to keep their wealth level hidden. Old money may be quieter than new money, perhaps, but as always beware of generalisations.

In situations when there are few other easily readable clues available about the underlying quality of a product or service, customers sometimes have rely upon price itself. Together with confirming indicators, such as branding and packaging, price is often taken as a very strong hint about what is the underlying quality of a product or service. Furthermore, since it is usually much more difficult to differentiate a service from competitors' offerings than it is to differentiate between products, many service providers use pricing as a key indicator of quality. Examples would include management consultants and top lawyers.

Tip

In the absence of other clues, there exist situations in which buyers will use price routinely as an indicator of quality. Builders provide an example, where quoting the lowest price will not always win you the sale. It is most certainly possible in business to be too cheap.

Price matters, but so does every opportunity to differentiate key features of your business's offering in your customers' eyes, highlighting features and attributes that set the product or service apart from its rivals. It then becomes possible to link price levels to the factors that make your offering different, or unique, or indeed to turn things around in order to use price levels as part of the differentiation process itself. When marketing material uses words like 'reassuringly expensive', it says it all.

Tip

Explain in your business plan how your business can achieve differentiation from its rivals, and then, using evidence from your market research, follow up by explaining how much of a premium your customers are prepared to pay, or how much of a discount they will expect, for those special features.

Launch pricing

For new businesses, and for new product or service lines, launch discounts and special promotions can play a key role as part of carefully formulated marketing strategies. Lower prices are often set at launch in order to win market share. Care is needed, however, since re-building price levels to where they need to be in economic terms can present problems.

If demand remains price sensitive, then the balance of power may have been moved to buyers from the seller and thus have a large detrimental effect upon long term profit potential. There always exists an infinite level of demand for a free product or service that customers want, and so selling something too cheaply may also generate demand levels greater than your business can accommodate, and cause damage to your business's reputation by harming customer goodwill.

However, where a business offering is in two related parts, computer printers and ink cartridges, for example, or razors and razorblades, then it may be possible to sell what is the more expensive element quite cheaply, but then generate the profits from selling the less expensive part rather dearly.

Cutting prices, sometimes called discounting or low-balling, in order to win market share, also risks starting a vigorous price-cutting war with rivals, who may possess greater financial muscle and management resources. Competition based upon price alone tends to damage all players in an industry in the longer term, because, as Porter's Five Forces model indicates, the profit available in that industry will shrink as the balance of power shifts. Buyers are able to spend less in that sector and thus benefit at the expense of sellers.

How much profit?

Three variables act to determine how much profit a product or service makes. These are the selling price itself, of course, the volume of sales achieved, and the underlying costs involved. These three factors are connected, since price levels directly affect sales volumes, generally the lower the price, the higher the volume. Secondly, sales volumes affect costs, since the effects of economies of scale in purchasing and in production are that costs per individual unit fall as volumes increase. Finally, cost levels are themselves a consideration, though as we have seen certainly not the only one, when setting sales prices.

The link between price levels and profits via sales volumes is direct and immediate. As reduced price levels increase sales volumes, that volume increase must be large enough to compensate for the reduction in profit made from each individual unit sold. Conversely, as higher prices cause sales volumes to fall, it is possible that the additional profit per unit can actually generate a greater profit in overall terms.

Price levels and profitability

The link between sales price, sales volumes and profit can be a very dramatic one.

For a business that achieves 40 per cent gross profit margins, for example, a two per cent price reduction requires that sales become boosted by five per cent as a result, just for that business to make the same level of gross profit as before. The table below shows just how dramatic this effect can be. A ten per cent price cut, for example, would need to generate a 33 per cent increase in sales volumes simply to ensure that the business made the same amount of gross profit.

Percentage *reduction* in selling price:	2	3	4	5	10	15
Percentage increase needed in sales volume:	5	8	11	14	33	60

Figure 6.1

In fact, a 20 per cent reduction in sales price would require that sales *double* to achieve the same level of gross profit.

The stark message is that reducing prices to win business may be a dangerous decision, since it can then require a much higher increase in sales volumes to be generated to allow the business to remain in the same place financially. Businesses that compete on price alone, or which become embroiled in price wars with competitors, ignore this effect at their peril.

On the other hand, raising prices may cause a drop-off in sales volumes, but even though that fall may turn out to be a higher percentage than the price increase, the business may still be able to make as much gross profit. The table below illustrates this, again using as an example a business that is presently making a 40 per cent gross profit margin.

Percentage *increase* in selling price:		2	3	4	5	10	15
Percentage decrease acceptable in sales volume:	5	7	9	11	20	27	

Figure 6.2

If that business were to raise prices by ten per cent, it could afford to suffer a fall in sales volumes of up to 20 per cent. Even with 20 per cent fewer sales, it would still make the same level of gross profit overall. In your business, the potential for raising prices should be food for thought, particularly if you want to avoid, or get away from, the busy fool syndrome in your business. That term is often used of course for people who find themselves working harder and harder simply for their businesses to remain in the same place financially.

Tip

Unless yours is a business providing a commodity product or service that it is virtually impossible to differentiate from rivals' offerings, do not compete on price alone. Find ways of enhancing your business's offering in your customers' eyes so that it can justify premium prices.

The tables above contain important lessons about the dangers that arise from cutting prices, and also about the potential benefits to businesses that can find ways of raising them. In the chapter on business finance this same point will be reinforced by using a worked example to demonstrate the effects.

Pricing strategies based upon costs

As we noted at the start of this chapter, the pricing of a product or a service must always have roots based in a business's cost structure. There are two pricing strategies commonly employed by businesses that are based upon cost levels: the cost-plus method, and marginal costing.

Cost-plus

The cost-plus method is exactly that, a mark-up, usually expressed as a percentage, added to the cost price of a product or service. This approach is commonly used in retail businesses, where standard mark-ups of, say, 100 or 200 per cent might be applied. Cost-plus is simple method to understand, and is easily used, but it has inherent failings as a pricing mechanism in some situations. It does not, for example, take into account customers' perceptions of the value of the business offering, other than in the very broadest terms where more up-market retailers will apply higher mark-up percentages than less expensive outlets.

The simple broad-brush approach of cost-plus also takes no account of the levels of demand between related product lines. The owner of a shop may find that all green jumpers have been sold, while the shelves remain fully stocked with blue jumpers, otherwise identical in all respects. The blue ones carry no higher mark-up, but remain unsold simply as a result of fashions in colour leading to a lower demand. Management can solve this problem by cutting prices on the slower-selling lines. The price reduction must to be sufficient to encourage buyers to purchase the less popular blue jumpers.

> ## Tip
>
> Customers are not interested in your business's cost structure, they are interested in the benefits, the value, the problem-resolution, that purchasing your product or service provides for them. Their question is simply whether the price that they are required to pay for the value they perceive makes the purchase decision a rational one for them.

Note that round sum cost-plus percentage mark-ups do not take much account of competitors' price levels either, except in the broadest terms, nor do they reflect the fact that some of the business's underlying costs will not vary with the volume of sales. Economies of scale affect input costs for what are referred to as variable costs, raw materials and labour costs, for example, but will not affect what are known as fixed costs, such as a shop's expenditure on rent. These terms are explained in more detail below. As noted above, these effects can produce a circular relationship between sales prices, sales volumes, and falling or rising costs per unit.

We will now turn to the vital area of understanding business cost behaviour patterns as we look at marginal costing.

Marginal costing

The second commonly encountered pricing mechanism is called marginal costing.

Marginal costing involves looking at the so-called marginal sale, the next item, and determining the level of costs that apply 'at the margin'. This means identifying the additional costs that will be incurred in producing and delivering that next item.

This method is more complex than the cost-plus, but marginal costing calculations can produce some very helpful data on which to base business pricing decisions. The method contains inherent dangers, however, and has to be used with care.

To illustrate how marginal costing is used in the real world, imagine a situation where a printing business has the opportunity to win a large, one-off sale, outside of its normal day-to-day activity levels.

Over the long run, in order to generate a profit in overall terms, a business must be able to generate total sales revenues that exceed its total costs. Total costs comprise those that are known as overheads, fixed costs or indirect costs, and those that are referred to as variable or direct costs.

This area is covered in more detail in the finance chapter of this book, but in broad terms the 'fixed' costs for a printer of being in business include costs such as the rent of business premises, administrative staff salaries, and the costs of the external accountants who prepare the accounts each year. In other words, the types of costs that are present in any event, regardless of whether any sales are made or not.

On the other hand, 'direct' business costs are those costs that are incurred specifically in producing individual print-jobs, and these direct costs increase or decrease, vary, therefore, depending upon sales levels. For a printing business, the major variable costs would be the costs of paper and inks.

Let's say that the printing business achieves a profit each month when its sales exceed £70,000. The business's usual pricing method involves costing each potential order, then supplying quotations to customers. To produce accurate costings, the printing press running time required is estimated, depending upon the nature and complexity of the individual job, then costed, using standard pre-set hourly rates. Anticipated printing press running time is thus used as the mechanism for allocating costs to potential orders.

In addition to the costs arising from, or rather allocated via, printing press running time, the company adds to each quotation the expected direct costs for the paper and inks that would be needed to produce the job, and then applies a percentage mark-up on top for profit. The level of that mark-up varies considerably, and to a large extent will be based upon the maximum selling price that the sales representative believes will be acceptable to the customer, based on each rep's detailed knowledge of that customer.

For normal day-to-day print jobs, quoted for when the factory is busy, the cost-plus method outlined above can be effective. It is essential that the cost figures applied to anticipated printing press time are reviewed frequently so that they reflect up-to-date business costs. Estimates of the amount of press running time needed for a print job must also be made as accurately as possible.

To allocate business costs to each hour of printing press time, assumptions will be needed, in particular the total number of hours that the press will be in operation each month. That allows total business costs to be allocated over the correct number of available printing hours. It is worth noting here that the need to make these assumptions ensures that what at appears to be an objectively scientific costing process actually contains areas within it that require estimates to be made.

Marginal costing techniques come into their own when the normal day-to-day situation does not apply. For example, a situation might arise where a potential order for a large quantity of travel brochures arrives on a Friday, with a deadline for delivery to the customer before 9 a.m. the following Monday morning. The printing business does not normally run a weekend production shift.

Using the company's normal cost-plus method, the sales rep produces a quotation of £12,000, which the customer subsequently rejects. The customer states, however, that they have budgeted for a maximum print cost of £10,000.

Should the company reject this potential order, therefore? Probably not. This large additional print job, this marginal job, is well suited to the use of a marginal costing approach. The sales director would need to step in and identify those costs that would be incurred directly in producing that specific order, which means those variable costs that arise only if that job was printed, including paper and ink costs, and printers' wages including any overtime payments for weekend working. Depending upon the size of the potential print-run, those marginal costs might also include an estimate of the additional wear and tear on the printing press itself.

This marginal costing approach would therefore determine the total variable costs for the job, the marginal costs, and compare those with the maximum price that the customer was willing to pay. If it happened that marginal costs would total £7,500, then by accepting the order at the £10,000 price at which it is available (or the customer would simply go elsewhere), the company is able to make a contribution towards its central overhead costs and profits of £2,500.

In other words, by accepting the marginal order at the lower-than-full-cost-plus price, the business would be able to generate £2,500 more contribution by Monday than if it simply rejected the order being available at a figure lower than its normal costings.

Other factors are relevant as well

In the real world, non-financial factors would also come into consideration. For example, if the print job in question might otherwise be won by a key competitor, that factor must have an influence. That influence would be greatest if the potential customer were a new one that held a potential for further work, or an existing one, until now loyal to the business. The sales director would be very aware of the need to ensure that the rival did not obtain an opportunity to establish a working relationship with a key customer.

One of the factors that made marginal costing relevant in this example was the availability of printing press capacity. It would not make financial sense, all other things being equal, for the company to accept an order won at a price level that arose from using marginal costing techniques to the detriment of a job that could be won after pricing it using a full-cost basis. If winning a marginally costed job resulted in a another job that needed to be on the presses at the same time having to be turned away, and that second job was available at a price that reflected full costs, then in comparative terms using marginal costs to set price would have led to a relative financial loss to the business.

If, on the other hand, the printing press was not busy, and would otherwise remain unused because no other print jobs were scheduled to run, then marginal costing techniques would be applicable, and could be used to justify accepting a lower price for a job that would otherwise be lost. By having an understanding of the principles involved, and having the figures available to make the calculations, the sales director could ensure that an otherwise idle press would at least make a contribution to overhead costs and profit, rather than generating no revenue at all.

Tip

Ensure that you understand fully your business's cost structure, and that you know accurately for any given sales volume both the full per unit cost of production, and the method for calculating marginal costs of production. That knowledge will provide you with the back-up information you need when setting prices. Understanding when to use cost-plus for pricing decisions, and when marginal costing techniques might be applicable, will provide you with a competitive price flexibility that your rivals may well not possess.

A slippery slope

A major risk exists for the unwary, and for the desperate, when their businesses stray into using a marginal cost approach to pricing for not just the above-normal orders, the one-offs, the orders when spare production capacity exists, but for normal day-to-day sales.

Tip

Be very watchful if you are often tempted to use marginal costing methods. Unless a business can cover all of its costs over the long run, then it will fail financially. If sales prices reflect only direct costs and variable costs, and do not cover an appropriate share of business overheads, then losses will pile up. Sales volumes may be sustained for a while, acting as a temporary smokescreen, a short-term palliative, but cash outflows triggered by the trading losses will eventually bankrupt the business.

Customer segmentation

Your marketing activities will be more successful if you are able to focus them with precision at specific targeted buyer groups, different customer segments that have different needs and different purchasing habits.

Even where that does not apply and a customer base is relatively homogenous in nature, it is quite likely that there exist a relatively small number of key accounts, star customers.

These will be the ones that are easiest to service, who place the biggest orders, and who settle their bills on time. This group is likely to be high in importance but few in number, and the major customers within it will probably warrant individual attention at senior level. Regular informal contact and staying very close to your customers will always build loyalty.

Marketing practice

The real-world examples that follow reveal how marketing theory and marketing practice join up in the real world.

The need to differentiate your business offering from your rivals' products and services is the emphasis in this section of your business plan. The comments set out below illustrate the ways in which real businesses seek to differentiate themselves from their rivals. The industry in this example is a particularly competitive one, domestic building and maintenance work. It is also one in which the business offering is often at or around commodity level, rebuilding a brick garden wall, for example, making it more difficult for individual businesses to differentiate their services from others.

The list has been compiled from comments made by owners of real-world businesses in this very competitive sector. Words in [square] brackets have been inserted to highlight some of the main marketing issues.

- 'We focus upon profitable work [markets] that is difficult to get into [high entry barriers], such as public sector [niche] work, where in order to get onto a local authority tender list businesses must be long-established and financially sound.'
- 'We know what we're good at and always emphasise that and our technical specialisations. [differentiation]. We reassure customers [we know what they want to buy] by explaining in detail the key technical requirements of the job. By showing that we understand these we are saying "look we have the expertise to cope"'.'
- 'We ... see ourselves as educating our customer so they get peace of mind [knowing what they are buying] in commissioning our business to do work.'
- 'We use past customers as references for new ones [differentiation]. We maintain a portfolio of photographs to show to prospects, and tell them to contact satisfied customers to take away the fear factor.'
- 'We never get into a bidding war after we have quoted a price for a job [pricing]. Our refusal to budge [differentiation] impresses customers, since we are actually saying that we are quality-based, not corner-cutters [differentiation].'
- 'We highlight our professional qualifications and are member of professional and trade bodies [differentiation]'
- 'We don't ignore what our rivals take for granted and don't even notice [differentiation]. That includes having smart company workwear with a logo and our motto, and clean vans. All of these get us noticed by customers as a quality firm.'
- 'Depending upon the size and complexity of the job, we aim to take time to get to know our potential customer and their individual needs.'

A customer is for life, or not

Another example, also drawn from the real world, highlights the differences in marketing approach between two businesses that provide professional advisory services to their customers. They refer to these customers as clients, but they are customers nonetheless.

The first business adopts a low-profile approach to marketing itself and its services, it does not concentrate many resources into activities that would lead to the recruitment of new customers. It believes that a customer is for life, and knows from experience that loyal customers frequently spread the word by telling their friends and business contacts. Existing satisfied customers form a fundamental part of the business's marketing effort.

The business's central philosophy is that customers remain loyal as long as they are looked after well, not subjected to frequent price increases, nor invoiced for every single telephone call. The average length of the business's customer retention period exceeds seven years.

The second business adopts a different approach to customers and their needs. It focuses corporate resources, both time and money, on numerous up-front marketing activities and initiatives. The business distributes expensively produced glossy brochures, maintains a comprehensive interactive website, and hosts breakfast clubs and technical seminars on a frequent basis. It seeks to differentiate itself from its lower-profile rival through its more prominent approach and by hosting seminars that effectively emphasise its technical expertise. Its areas of expertise are in fact exactly on a par with the first business, but that is not how its customers perceive things.

The second business's senior employees are often found out in the business community, wining and dining their contacts and clients, and being busy at business and charitable functions. It charges more for each hour of its expertise than does its competitor, and concentrates targeted effort into wooing specific customers away from its rival. If it succeeds it sees the new opportunity as a short-term one, and thus will invoice new customers as much as possible. As a result within two or three years many new customers will have moved on again, either to a new supplier entirely, or back to the first firm.

Both of these business models exist, and each can be found in the real world supplying professional financial services. The two firms are broadly equivalent in terms of profitability. The second business generates higher revenues, but spends much more on front-end customer recruitment activities, and on the post-delivery time needed justifying some of the higher bills to its customers.

The first business spends little on building its profile, but it retains customers for much longer period. Its customers often appreciate their position of power, however, not least by the wooing they receive from the second firm. Many have learned, therefore, to express vociferously their sensitivity to increased prices; in the business relationship customers hold the balance of power by the implicit threat of leaving. As a direct consequence, the first business often finds it difficult to raise prices for existing customers when it needs to.

These are different business models, and both are successful. The first is based upon a broad philosophy of securing long-term customer loyalty, customers for life. The second is relying on high front-end expenditure in order to secure the recruitment of new customers, but then making as much money, legitimately, from those customers for as long as they stick around, and generating a higher level of customer throughput as a result.

For the second business, customer inertia, an imperfection in the market caused by human behaviour, allied with a degree of difficulty for customers in seeing easily what the low-profile business's price levels are, added also to the human tendency to equate quality with price in terms of professional services, ensures continued strong revenue streams.

Your business's position

If yours was a professional services business, would your marketing efforts focus on securing a customer for life, or at least for more than a single purchase? Or would they lean more towards maximising the short-term returns? It may sound crude, but many businesses rely on the maximisation of one-off customer hits, whether they consciously appreciate that fact or not. Or, in different market segments, does your business have the potential to pursuing both of these strategies for maximum sales effect?

Out of all business plan areas, it is marketing that most often receives its own dedicated sub-plan, giving this area the major attention that it merits. As was said earlier, without customers, a business is nothing.

The professional services example was designed to make the point that fundamentally different approaches can work for competing players within the same industry and segment. These differences in approaches are themselves a means of differentiation, of course.

Your business's approach to marketing issues may lie in the nature of its product or service. Would customers return, again and again, given the chance, even if the interval was of a few years? Costs of retaining customers would be low in that situation, and a business might choose to adopt something approaching the first business model above as having much to commend it. Legal firms carrying out property conveyancing services might fit that mould rather well.

However, for a business that was likely to see a client just once, the strategy with the best chance of maximising sales and profits might well be the second one, that of invoicing the customer for as much as possible. Some people who have been through the process might believe that such a strategy was sometimes employed by lawyers in the divorce industry. In their defence, not that they need it, divorce lawyers are, of course, under an obligation to achieve the very best result for each client. The divorce process is itself a highly complex process at many levels, which demands time and the highest levels of legal expertise to handle correctly.

Competitors

If you have identified a new idea that will meet customers' needs better, or you have found a new way of doing existing things in ways that better meet customers' needs, be aware that it is very hard to run a successful business and yet remain invisible.

Any competitive advantage that you can establish will diminish over time, as it becomes eroded by the forces of competition. That erosion may be rapid, or gradual, depending upon the size and nature of your business's advantage, and the nature and extent of the barriers to entry in the industry in which your business operates. Your task for your business is to be able to sustain your competitive advantage, and your business's marketing activities are its front line of defence in many ways.

Conclusion

The marketing section of your business plan poses a real challenge, it is often the most difficult one to do really well. A strong business plan outlines a detailed marketing model for a business. Yours must talk about defined customers whose needs your business offering has been tailored to meet in unique ways. Those ways should reflect your customers' needs, and the various types of profit opportunity that they represent. Inevitably, that also means analysing your rivals thoroughly as well. Do not leave a big gap.

The questions to address are not just how your business's offering will be different, but how will your customers know that it is different and the benefits that brings them? And how much will they pay for those benefits?

Investment of the time necessary to get the marketing elements right will produce a number of opportunities to improve your business's chances of success:

- You will gain the opportunity to fine-tune key features of your product or service, or even to completely redesign your offering in order to match customers' needs even more closely.
- You can decide exactly how best to inform your desired customers about your business's offering, and its specific benefits.
- You will be at the correct starting point to design a targeted marketing plan. That will place your business ahead of rivals who start their marketing strategy from the point called 'how can I try to let my vaguely defined customers know about the very-interesting-to-me features of my product or service that I imagine that they will want?'. That said, never underestimate your rivals either; confidence is good, but arrogance is just asking for trouble.
- You can make decisions about the operational processes needed to produce your product or service. 'I now know that my customers' needs are these, so what are the ways in which my business can produce and deliver its offering at least cost?' You can also remove features of your present offering that are neither needed nor significantly valued by your customers. If that sounds like deciding which corners can be cut with no detriment to the business, then that is exactly what the business re-engineering process represents. Corner-cutting is not a pejorative term in this context, since you would be removing specific attributes that add little or no value in your customers' eyes.
- You can identify the most appropriate route(s) to market, meaning the ways in which customers can gain access to the product or service.

- Possibly most importantly of all in generating long-term business growth, once your business's offering exactly matches the needs of your customers, you can start to think about scalability. Does your business have a bigger potential? Might it be able to move into other related market segments, and attract to nearby customer groups?

Pricing matters, and is itself an art form in many situations, backed up by some science from your business's financial costings. The approach to pricing that will impress readers of your business plan is the one that comes from demonstrating a customer's-eye view of your offering. That customer's-eye view includes customers' imperfect view of your rivals' prices for direct competitor products and services and for substitutes.

Here is a helpful final thought. After they have grown large, and become diverse in their range of activities, it is often rather difficult to see the point from which successful businesses started out. Most began simply, however, meeting the needs of a small group of customers very well indeed, and then they built outwards in small steps from that point. Those steps may well have been rapid, but they were unlikely to have been gigantic leaps. Each step repeated what worked before, with alert and nimble management discarding errors as they occurred, and taking the lessons forward.

Your business should focus on meeting customers' needs, delivering the goods, and then you start building it outwards from there.

INSTANT TIP

Unless yours is a business providing a commodity product or service that is virtually impossible to differentiate from your rivals' offerings, never compete on price alone.

07

The finances: how do I learn to understand the numbers and use them to support my business case?

Managers thinking about accounting issues should never forget one of Abraham Lincoln's favorite riddles: 'How many legs does a dog have if you call his tail a leg?' The answer: 'Four, because calling a tail a leg does not make it a leg'.

Warren Buffet

He who asks may be a fool for five minutes, but he who doesn't ask remains a fool forever.

Chinese proverb

Introduction

Running any business requires an understanding of the principles of business finance, but for many people the place called finance is a blind spot. This chapter covers the essentials. If you have no prior knowledge of business finance, or if you are simply unsure about how much you do know, this chapter will guide you from the point of view of the financial knowledge needed to produce a business plan.

> **Tip**
>
> The financial elements of your business plan on their own will not be enough to make it succeed, but they may certainly be enough to make it fail. Financial information prepared well is always expected. Financial information prepared badly will ensure that credibility is lost more rapidly than in any other part of your plan.

Accounts in the UK follow standard formats, and once you have made yourself familiar with those, and understand what they show, then you possess the potential to be able to read any set of accounts. This chapter explains the structure of the main business accounting statements, and why professional accountants produce business accounts in the ways that they do.

It is worth saying that business finance can appear daunting, and that many people are not confident when using the language of accountancy. This problem is compounded by some within the financial profession, who wield the jargon but are unable, or possibly sometimes unwilling, to explain financial matters simply for the uninitiated. It is not just business owners and managers who need to analyse business financial performance either. There are many other interested groups, including investors, employees, suppliers, customers, and HM Revenue & Customs.

The jargon problem occurs in many situations. Groups of people with common interests – military personnel, marketing specialists, lawyers, computer experts – all develop their own argot. A specialist language will always have a practical role within the group, but also builds something of a mystique, keeping outsiders at bay. Quite possibly there are both employment and business situations where that helps to keep prices up for the continuing benefit of the insiders.

An extra layer of complexity exists, however, for jargon from the world of business finance, in that it comes with figures attached. Many more people prefer dealing with words rather than numbers. Even some individuals directing larger businesses have not really got to grips with business finances earlier in their careers, and eventually those people are promoted to such heights that they are no longer able to admit to financial blind spots.

Tip

If you aren't sure about something, ask. Arm yourself with a competent accountant who can and will explain things, Then ask again until you are sure. Being caught out on the finances is probably the most efficient way of ensuring that would-be backers lose confidence. They may not be professional accountants any more than you are, but they will most certainly understand the fundamentals, which means being able to identify and challenge the critical numbers for any business.

The two main difficulties in understanding business finance

Understanding business finance means getting past the language barrier and being as relaxed when reading the accounting numbers, the financial statements, as you are when you read words and diagrams. Finance is central to all aspects of business, so if you cannot achieve a level of basic confidence then your management vision will have a large blind spot right in the middle of it.

When you first learned to read you would soon have coped with simple, short sentences. By the time you were seven or eight years old you could probably read with some confidence, but would not have been able, or indeed have wished, to read James Joyce. To read accounts at the essential level for general financial competence requires only the equivalent of the story reading ability of a seven-year-old. You just need to make sense of things by understanding the key vocabulary, the financial jargon, and how the overall structure fits together.

That part of financial understanding is less difficult than it can seem at first. You do not need to reach the accounts equivalent of *Ulysses*. You need only be at or around the accounts equivalent of *Things to See at the Seaside*.

After an initial reluctance then, many people find then that the big problem with business finance lies not in getting to grips with the basics, that much can be accomplished quite quickly. The problem occurs later, since accounts come with a twist in the tail. Having determined to gather some financial knowledge, it is quite possible to work your way through the basics only to find that when you try to apply your new-found knowledge in the real world you become bogged down, stuck in the detail.

As a result you remain unable to see an overall view, the hilltop remains shrouded in mist. It may well be a glorious sunny day above cloud level, but the view from where you are standing is obscured by a pea-souper and at best you can see only a small way in any direction.

This chapter explains the essential jargon, and does so in a way that provides you with a framework of understanding for business finance as a whole, a way of beginning to see the bigger view. It is gaining that bigger perspective that will allow you to focus on details as needed. Your goal in finance is to be able to move smoothly from broad review of the big picture down to precise focus, from overview to detailed inspection of areas that warrant your managerial attention. That is the art of reading business accounts.

Although it takes many years of real-world experience to become a financial expert, there exist a small number of financial techniques that are relatively easy to understand, and those are the ones that will be outlined here to enable you to produce the financial parts of your business plan.

Limitations of business accounts

A good starting place is to dispel a few common misunderstandings, to explain what accounts can do and what they cannot.

First, accounts only measure those aspects of business activities that can be measured readily. Conventional accounts do not measure the value of all business assets, for example, such as the dedication, loyalty and general level of morale of employees. In fact, for people and knowledge-based businesses it can readily be argued that the largest asset of all, the workforce, is not valued at all in conventional accounting terms. Another gap may be that environmental costs, particularly longer-term ones, are not brought into the reckoning by conventional business accounts.

The problem lies not so much with the ability of finance and accounts to handle, for example, a measure of morale, it lies with an inability to obtain that measurement in a way that would stand up to objective scrutiny. In general, accounts measure only those things that can be measured in financial terms, and things that can be measured on the short- to medium-term time horizon. Thus, although it is rather difficult to place an objective valuation upon the level of employee knowledge, or skill, or loyalty within a business, in situations where such a measure is readily available then accounts will accommodate it easily. Football club accounts do it as a matter of course when it comes to the costs of signing players, for example.

Business accounts have a few limitations at the edges then, but at the core of accounting expertise and accounting practice there exist techniques that are extremely useful to support business decision-making. Accounting and financial techniques allow management to ensure the financial health and well-being of their businesses, and determine what funding resources are needed, and when. They enable management to monitor progress against targets, to measure and improve business efficiency, and to optimise utilisation of the limited resources available.

The essentials

Once you have mastered the basic business financial jargon, you can start using the data provided by business accounts to supply useful management information. The next point has previously been mentioned, but is so important that it now receives a second airing. Having access to an accountant who speaks in plain English is a very valuable resource indeed, and it is worth investing time to locate one. Ask around for recommendations, and do not necessarily rely on impressively gloss brochures or a comprehensive website, for such things can easily be purchased and simply re-branded with a given firm's name.

Tip

Meet the individual who would be your day-to-day contact, check that the personal chemistry works, and check whether they can explain financial matters in ways that you understand. A good test here is a practical one: ask them to explain how your business's accounts would show things if a computer were purchased, for example. Do you understand their explanation?

The three main financial statements

The principal accounting statements are these:

- The profit and loss account, which shows the amount of profit or loss that a business has produced, or expectations of what it is forecast to produce, for a stated period.
- The balance sheet, which shows the business's assets and its liabilities as they exist at a fixed point. How much are funds in the bank, for example, and how much is owed to the business by its debtors, anyone who owes it money.
- The cashflow forecast, which shows expectations of when cash funds will be received by a business, and when it will be paid out, measured against a timeline.

Profit and loss account

The accounting statement that people most readily understand is the profit and loss account. It is an account, a reckoning up, of whether a business, or an individual departmental unit within a larger business, has made a profit or not. The very straightforward logic is that if all revenues for a given period are added up, that provides the total income earned figure for that period. A parallel totalling process carried out for costs, the various items of expenditure incurred during the same period, gives the total costs figure.

Setting the first total against the second is the essence of a business profit and loss account. If total revenues exceed total costs then a profit has been achieved, if costs exceed revenue then a loss has been incurred.

Understanding what a profit and loss account is, and what it shows, is not complicated therefore. The issue that often confuses people, however, is the question of timing. At what point is it correct for a business to claim to have generated a sale, to have generated revenue? When the customer pays the invoice? When the business originally raised it?

The answer is that accounting practice follows the legal position, and if you remember this point then the principle should stick in your mind. Quite simply, a business will recognise a sale as having happened, record it as revenue earned and take credit for it, once there exists a legally binding obligation upon the customer to pay. That point is generally the point at which the product or service has been successfully delivered, or otherwise provided to the customer's satisfaction.

Exactly the same principle applies when recognising the existence of business costs as having been incurred. Costs are recognised, and a financial liability to suppliers is recorded, as soon as there comes into existence a legally binding obligation to make payment to the supplier.

The accounting treatment for both income and costs follows the same underlying principle. Both sales revenues, often called 'turnover' in the jargon, and costs, are recorded as soon as a legally binding obligation to pay comes into existence. It does not matter at all from a profit and loss account viewpoint when payment is actually received or made; all that matters is recording revenues when these are earned, and recording liabilities for business for costs as these are incurred.

In summary, a profit and loss account measures whether a business has made a profit or not by setting costs incurred against revenues earned. Both costs and revenue are recorded when legally binding obligations to pay come into existence, not when the payments happen. There is indeed another business financial statement that concerns itself with the timing of movements of funds in and out of a business, when liabilities to suppliers have to be paid, and when customers are expected to pay their debts. That is known as the cashflow statement, and will be dealt with later in this chapter.

Hedgefrogs Limited: fixed costs and variable costs

To help users of accounts, accountants segregate costs into specific categories, fixed or variable, according to the way in which they behave. This is the same principle as that explained in the previous chapter when looking at pricing a product or service using marginal costing techniques.

Hedgefrogs Limited manufactures two lines of boot scrapers that remove mud, Herbert Hedgehog and Doris the Frog, and it operates from a rented former agricultural building. Hedgefrogs' accountant categorises the business costs into two categories, those incurred in actually making the products, the variable costs, and those that exist anyway, regardless of whether any products are made or not, the fixed costs or overheads.

Variable costs comprise the costs of raw materials: wood, blocks of bristles, varnish, eyes, noses, screws and glue, plus the wages costs of the people who produce the boot scrapers. These variable costs, the ones that relate directly to making the business's product, are also known as direct costs. They vary, rise or fall, in direct proportion to the number of hedgefrogs produced.

The business incurs its fixed costs or overheads in any event, regardless of whether any scrapers are produced, or none at all. These costs do not vary with production levels. Rental costs for the company's premises fall into this category, since the company entered into a contractual liability to its landlord as soon as the lease for premises was signed. The rental charge will not change in the short term, no matter whether the production line is busy or completely idle.

Examples of costs normally treated as being fixed in an accounting context include advertising expenditure, printing and stationery costs, wages for administrative staff, and the costs of maintaining a website. The point is that such costs are not fixed by virtue of anything other than the fact that they do not vary directly with production levels. They can and will vary in amount, for example, if a new advertising campaign is mounted in order to generate additional sales.

In reality in fact all costs vary over time. A growing business might need to rent additional premises, for example. To reiterate the fixed or variable categorisation of costs by accountants in the profit and loss account is based upon whether an item of expenditure varies with production levels.

Confusion sometimes arises also because beyond a certain point a precise classification of cost behaviour may be impossible. Accountants are then forced to use best judgement when classifying costs as fixed or variable.

To illustrate the point, assume that the manager of the boot scraper business spent approximately (it will never be exact) 90 per cent of their time on the production line actually making products, and the rest in carrying out more general managerial tasks. In that situation the accountant might well decide to allocate the owner's employment costs in the profit and loss account on a pro-rata basis, allocating 90 per cent under the direct/variable costs heading, and the remaining ten per cent as overheads/fixed costs. That method would ensure that the direct costs of producing boot scrapers included the costs of the manager's time when working on production, but excluded the time devoted to non-production activities.

It could also be argued, however, that all of the manager's salary was a fixed cost to the business, incurred in any event in the short run, irrespective of whether scrapers were produced or not. The decision to use a 90/10 split of management wages costs is therefore driven by the accountant's judgement. The important issue being which treatment of management wages would most accurately reflect the underlying cost structure of the business.

Cost classification looks like a precise science, but is not always so. It very often needs a degree of judgement to be applied. From the point of view of preparing your business plan, and of running your business successfully, what matters is gaining a broad understanding of the underlying principles of cost classification.

The following example illustrates why accountants categorise costs as variable or fixed. Classifying costs between ones that vary with sales and that do not lets managers make better business decisions.

Each boot scraper design sells for £11. Hedgefrogs' manager estimates that to produce 15,000 boot scrapers next quarter the following variable costs will be incurred:

Production wages	£23,000
Wood	£ 6,000
Bristle blocks	£15,000
Eyes and noses, screws, glue, varnish, etc.	£ 1,000

The company will also have fixed costs totalling £56,000 for rent, business rates, light and heat, administrative wages, and advertising.

Knowing which costs are fixed and which are variable permits the manager to make some simple but extremely useful calculations. Read the step-by-step calculations below, slowly, to ensure that you understand how each figure is arrived at.

1. Variable costs incurred in producing 15,000 boot scrapers will total £45,000, giving a variable cost per scraper of £3.
2. Since boot scrapers sell for £11, every one sold generates £8 above the variable costs of its production.
3. Each of those £8 amounts make a contribution towards the company's fixed costs of £56,000, and, when all of those have been covered, towards the business making a net profit after all of its costs have been covered.

Contribution is also known in the jargon as the gross profit, the profit made by a business before any of its fixed costs are taken into account.

Break-even analysis

The manager's forecasts show that the business's fixed costs for the next quarter will total £56,000, which allows a calculation to be made of exactly how many boot scrapers need to be sold in order for the business to break even. In other words, how many boot scrapers must be sold, each one making a contribution of £8, to generate enough contribution in total to cover the fixed costs of £56,000?

If each boot scraper generates a gross profit or contribution of £8, then sales of 7,000 boot scrapers during the next quarter would cover the business's fixed costs. Seven thousand units sold producing £8 contribution per unit produces a total contribution of £56,000. That figure would be sufficient to pay all of the business's fixed costs for the next quarter, leaving the business exactly at break even, making neither a profit nor a loss.

Here are two further questions:

1. If the business actually sold 10,000 boot scrapers during the next quarter, how much net profit would it make after fixed costs?

2. If, as a result of pressure from large garden centres' buyers, the average selling price achieved turned out to be only £10 per unit, how many scrapers would have to be sold in order for the business to break even?

The answers follow below, with explanations, but try to work them out for yourself before you check.

Some of the major benefits from the accountants' classification of costs behaviour have started to become visible. Separating variable costs from the fixed costs enables a business's break-even point to be calculated, as in the example above. Performing these calculations allows businesses not just to determine break-even point but also what profits or losses will be made at various sales volumes. That information can be used to run businesses better, in setting weekly or monthly targets for the sales teams, for example, and in designing sales teams' remuneration and commission structures in ways that incentivise sales achievements beyond break-even levels.

Devising meaningful sales targets is a first step, but note in passing they must be communicated effectively too. Managers can employ various devices which assist in their achievement, using visual aids, for example, that clearly portray progress made to date towards target. Charts, graphs, and other visual devices are much easier to comprehend quickly than tables of figures. Targets and progress towards thereby can be made clearly visible to the sales team and, most fundamentally of all, really mean something to the business.

In the real world many managers remain unaware of these quite simple calculations, let alone able to use them to run their businesses. Sales targets are frequently based on last year's figure plus X per cent, a widespread phenomenon that does not motivate sales teams well, not least because it has very little underlying meaning.

Solutions to boot scraper questions:

1. £24,000. This is calculated as sales of an additional 3,000 scrapers, each one producing a contribution to profit of £8. Note that all of the business's fixed costs have already been covered by the sales of the first 7,000 scrapers.

		£
Sales of 10,000 scrapers at £11 each		110,000
Costs of 10,000 scrapers at £3 each		30,000
Total gross profit contribution	80,000	
Less fixed costs	56,000	
Net profit	£ 24,000	

The answer can be proved the longer way round, equally valid, as follows:

2. 8,000 units. The gross profit or contribution per scraper has fallen to £7. Since fixed costs remain at £56,000, the business now needs to achieve sales of 8,000 units at £7 contribution each to cover its fixed costs.

Reducing prices

The previous chapter explained that reducing sales prices can be a high-risk strategy. In the example above, a reduction of £1 in the sales price, 1/11th, just over nine per cent, required a sales volume increase of 1,000 units, 1/7th, over 14 per cent, to compensate. That calculation highlights the difficulties that arise when businesses cut prices in order to stimulate flagging demand, and or find themselves embroiled in a price war with their rivals.

A reduction in sales price will require a higher increase in sales volumes. In percentage terms the extra sales volume needed by Hedgefrogs to stay in the same place financially is over 1.5 times greater than the price reduction, 14 per cent versus nine per cent. In a price war situation, where demand is essentially constant and therefore overall sales volumes cannot increase, the protagonists are simply reducing the overall amount of profit available to them.

Businesses that use reduced prices alone to shore up flagging demand often find themselves in a downward spiral as they chase customers. There is rarely any certainty that sales will be stimulated enough to rise by the extra volume needed to compensate, but customers' fundamental expectations may change. They may begin to expect ever lower prices. Consciously or unconsciously, customers perceive that the balance of power is shifting from the sellers towards them as buyers.

In terms of Porter's Five Forces model, customers find that they can retain more of the overall profit by negotiating shrewdly, and quite possibly by playing one supplier off against the next, making levels of price-cutting even more severe. The buyers' gains matches sellers' losses.

As we saw in the last chapter, there is some good news, however. If it can be achieved, the act of increasing sales prices by a percentage has the effect of requiring only a smaller percentage fall in sales volumes for the business to achieve the same result. Thus, if management is able to use marketing techniques to differentiate the business's offering, effectively locking in customers, so that the actual fall in the volume of sales is less than that, then more profit will be the result.

Profit and loss account layout

A standard profit and loss layout is as follows. In broad terms this summarised format is set out in the Companies Acts as being the one that all limited companies must adopt when producing their annual published accounts. Note that the jargon word for sales is turnover, and remember that direct costs is a synonym for variable costs:

	£
Turnover	A
Less: direct costs	(B)
Gross Profit	GP
Less: overheads	(O)
Net profit	NP

Figure 7.1

Cashflow statements

As explained earlier, the point at which a customer actually pays for a product or service is simply not relevant in profit and loss account terms. The position is that revenue and costs are recognised, accounted for, as soon as a legally binding obligation to pay comes into existence.

In complete contrast, cashflow statements show a business' financial position based upon when liquid funds, which are generally referred to as 'cash', actually move.

Businesses fail financially when they run out of cash to pay the bills. This point is enshrined in UK insolvency legislation for companies, that of not being able to pay business debts as they fall due, which effectively says the same thing. Most people associate insolvency with losses, but running out of cash to pay suppliers can happen even when trading is profitable.

For most businesses the normal situation is one of time-lag, where funds flow to pay suppliers before funds flow back in again from customers. The major exception to this is for retail businesses, where customers generally pay as they take away the goods or receive the service. For most businesses, however, receipts from customers occurs after a delay, with payments to suppliers falling due in advance of that. Even using the best debt-collection techniques, the period of that time-lag can be an uncertain and rather dangerous place.

Tip

Preparing a *forecast* cashflow statement for your business, updating it regularly in the light of events, and measuring actual performance against it together comprise the most important safeguards for ensuring the financial health of your business. If you are skimming this section and do nothing else, please hard-wire that last sentence into your memory. Cash is king. That might be very trite, but it is utterly true.

Well-managed businesses always focus on cash

Rapid business growth usually results in extreme pressures upon all operating areas, financial ones not least. In the early 1990s, not long after I had set up my chartered accountancy practice, I was recommended to a very rapidly growing business.

During an initial meeting with the owner, my objective was to learn how he saw his business developing and to understand his motivations and major objectives. I needed to know what he wanted to achieve from the business and within what timescale. I soon realised that I wanted to act for that individual, always my own golden rule. When we began to discuss the business's financial aspects, he explained in a slightly abashed way that he maintained a simple record-keeping system despite sales that were already well into six figures.

Then, extracted from a desk, was what turned out to be a very large spreadsheet. It was made up of many A4 pages joined together with sticky tape. Somewhat unwieldy though it was, that spreadsheet was perfection in its focus. It contained all of the important financial information about the business in a way that the owner understood and could use, notwithstanding the fact that he had received no formal financial training whatsoever.

The owner, Andy, had focused upon the movements of liquid funds in and out of the business, the cashflow, rather than upon the levels of profit. He knew that as long as he held a firm grasp of the amounts and timing of funds flowing in to the business, and micro-managed also the cash flowing out, then that information would allow him to see problems coming far enough ahead to safeguard the business's finances.

The best business school training simply could not have provided a more fundamental focus. The owner had determined what he needed, and had identified the holy grail of business finance, the very tight management of cashflow.

Tip

Manage the cashflows in your business. Do not be seduced by the levels of profit or by asset values, focus on the cashflow and the rest will follow much more easily. As noted already, businesses fail not simply because they make losses. It is quite common for businesses to fail despite the fact that they are generating a profit. *Businesses fail because when run out of cash*. It is that simple.

Understanding business cashflow

For most businesses, then, there exists a delay between funds flowing out and then flowing back in again. A few industries are exceptions to this rule, a clearly visible one being retail stores and supermarkets as noted above. Note in passing that in terms of Porter's Five Forces model the larger ones have sufficient buyer power to negotiate slow settlement terms with their suppliers. The rather more common situation, however, is the reverse. Suppliers, and that includes employees, the suppliers of business labour, must be paid before customers eventually settle their debts.

Ebb and flow

The cashflow cycle for a business, the movement of bank balances from day to day, is paralleled in many ways by the movement of waves on a beach. Cash in a business is sometimes referred to as liquid funds, and it is possible to liken business cash movements as waves of funds. Imagine yourself at a position close to the water's edge, a point representing the start of business activity. At that point, water is flowing away from you, in the same way that liquid funds move out of a business as it pays its suppliers. The next incoming wave brings more water to the beach, reflecting the funds flow into a business in due course as customers pay their debts. Funds will then flow back out again as more suppliers are paid.

As with waves on a beach, at any given time the tide will be coming in, or going out. In either event, the size of the incoming waves varies, sometimes the next wave will bring in less water than previously flowed out, sometimes more. Usually, outflows and inflows happen at the same time in fact, with incoming waves covering water flowing back out. A business will sometimes both receive cash from customers and pay out cash to its suppliers on the same day. In overall terms, over time, the tide of cashflow for a profitable business will be a rising one, the net situation being one where more cash flows in than flows out.

A beach metaphor works well for the movements of cash in a business, but you should appreciate that at the start point, the water's edge, the first wave may not be flowing towards you, it will probably be flowing out. That water flowing out comes from a previous inflow, which in business terms may mean the original capital injected into the business, or a bank overdraft facility that has been set up in advance to cope with the outflow of funds. However, it is very likely indeed if your business is a new one that your arrival at the water's edge does not just coincide with a wave ebbing back out, but with the whole tide on its way out, and with incoming waves being few and far between.

Even for successful businesses on a flood tide in terms of liquid funds, the tide will turn if trading takes a downturn, or if expansion and growth lead to larger amounts of cash being caught up in the time-lag, or if the acquisition of equipment or vehicles or buildings uses up a high proportion of the cash balances.

For new businesses, incurring trading losses during the initial stages, more cash will certainly be running out of the business than flows back in again from sales. When the business starts to make a profit at last, the tide should begin to turn. Water will always ebb as well as flow, though, because even when a tide is rising there will be occasions when the latest incoming wave is smaller than the previous outgoing one.

Note also that there is probably also a stream flowing onto this metaphorical business beach. That stream represents a business's fixed costs, the outflows of the liquid funds needed to pay the overhead costs. That stream is running out along the beach, regardless of the stage of tide, or what individual waves are doing. Fixed costs, overheads have that effect upon cash. To pay them, cash is always moving out of the business irrespective of the levels of sales.

The picture is now complete. Once a business is trading profitably in overall terms, the tide of liquid funds is coming in. Incoming and outgoing waves represent the cash generated from customers and the cash expended on paying suppliers for variable costs. Even when the tide is coming in there will be occasions when the previous wave running back out is greater in volume than the next wave arriving at the beach. Ebb and flow. Finally, the stream permanently flowing into the sea represents the outflows of cash needed to pay the business's fixed costs, the outflow of cash that is quite independent of what is happening to sales and variable costs.

How much funding is required?

Your business plan needs to include forecasts of the movements of liquid funds in and out of your business. The purpose of these business cashflow forecasts is to reveal anticipated peaks and troughs in the balances of liquid funds, and therefore to allow management to put sufficient funding resources into place, including short-term borrowings such as bank overdraft facilities, to be available to cope with the times of greatest outflow.

Using the beach metaphor, the volume of water in the stream that flows onto the beach, and its speed of flow, together with the size of the waves and the intervals between them all vary over time. As a business grows, so will its cashflows vary. In terms of your business plan, this is the point at which your business's overall funding requirement must be addressed. If your business needs external finance, then investors and bankers will need convincing that you have forecast its cash needs as accurately as possible.

The range of questions to consider is as follows:

- How much funding in total does the business need?
- When is it needed?

- How much is needed in the form of long-term finance, locked into the business to provide for equipment and infrastructure and development needs, and how much is needed as working capital to fund day-to-day trading activities?
- Is the long-term need such that it suits a long-term borrowing structure ('debt') or does it require share capital ('equity'), or a mixture of both? Where outside investors are involved they will need to see the size of the potential returns available to them, and over what timescale these are expected to arise
- What so-called 'milestones' are available in the business's progress, to be used as markers, the achievement of which allows funding arranged in principle to be drawn down into the business's bank account?

Tip

Your user-friendly accountant's expertise will be needed to help with some of these questions. The detailed financial elements of your plan, certainly in funding terms, will benefit considerably from professional guidance. Gaining a sound working understanding of business finance does *not* make you an expert in funding structures or funding sources.

The financial forecasts contained within your business plan provide the information that allows these questions to be answered.

Balance sheet

The third and final accounting statement is the balance sheet, which contains that 'balance' word so beloved of accountants. At its most fundamental level, a balance sheet sets out the assets that a business owns and against those sets its liabilities, the amounts that the business owes.

Some real-world business plans dispense with the need to include forecast balance sheets, not least where the business unit is a department within a larger business entity. If, however, your business's need is to raise significant amounts of funding, then you will almost certainly need to produce projected balance sheets. These will allow the types of funding needed to be determined, in terms of both amounts required and type, so that they best fit your business's anticipated needs.

> ## Tip
>
> As a minimum in business you should understand and feel confident in using the basic concepts underlying profit and loss accounts and cashflow forecasts. These are the minimum that every strong plan should include. Whether or not you will need to prepare forecast balance sheets as well depends to a large extent upon individual business plan circumstances.

If your business seeks significant external funding then you will need to produce balance sheets as well, and if you do not have some specialist financial background, your user-friendly accountant will be a great source of help here as well. That said, always ensure that you understand what a balance sheet is and what it shows.

Double-entry accounting

First and foremost, a balance sheet must always balance. That is because for several centuries accountants have employed an accounting technique referred to as double-entry accounting, which was invented by an Italian monk.

Double-entry bookkeeping is a skill that takes practitioners a long time to master, yet the underlying principle for the double-entry method is not complex at all. Each time that a transaction is recorded, posted into the accounting records of a business, it is entered twice, once on the 'debit' side, and once on the 'credit' side. It automatically follows that for any set of accounting entries, postings as they are known, at the end of any period of time, the total of the debit entries *must* equal the total of the credits. It is as simple as that. The key point being that double-entry accounting is self-balancing, which means self-checking.

The need to use a double-entry system of bookkeeping arises from simple human fallibility. In any single-entry bookkeeping system, in which each business transaction was entered only once in the accounting records, a lapse of concentration by a bookkeeper could cause an incorrect figure to be entered, or two digits to be entered the wrong way around, transposing them. Such all-too-human errors could remain undetected unless each individual entry was checked.

The double entry system, on the other hand, seeks to ensure that errors come to light because the two totals, one of all the debit entries and one of all the credits, will not then be the same. They will not balance, in fact. Note finally the double-entry system is not completely foolproof that even, however, since it is just possible that a compensating error, identical in amount, is also made in such a way that the second error cancels out the first. This is unlikely in reality but not impossible.

Every business balance sheet is derived from the double-entry method's fundamental balancing process. Each shows the various assets of the business at a given point, and reveals also its liabilities at that same point. As we saw earlier, a profit and loss account is drawn up to show trading results for the whole of a stated period: a month, a quarter, a year, but a key difference with a balance sheet is that it is produced to show assets and liabilities in existence at a single point. A balance sheet would thus be headed up, for example, 'Hedgefrogs Limited Balance Sheet as at 30 June 20XX'.

> ## Tip
> The fact is that a balance sheet is drawn up at a stated point becomes rather obvious when you realise that by the next trading day the asset and liability situation may well have changed.

For example, Hedgefrogs Limited's balance sheet at 30 June might show that the amounts owed by various debtors, customers for boot scrapers, totalled £28,000. If on 1 July customers purchased an additional £5,000-worth of boot scrapers, and on that same day also payments were received from debtors totalling £3,000, then the debtor balance at close of play on 1 July would be £30,000, a net total of £2,000 higher.

A balance sheet shows, therefore, what is frequently referred to as a snapshot of the assets and liabilities of the business at the stated point in time at which it is drawn up. By showing the assets at that point, and by deducting the liabilities at the same point, the balance sheet also reveals the total net assets of the business, the amount that the business owes back to its owners.

That net asset figure is also the figure as the capital of the business, another automatic balance brought about by the way in which the double-entry method works. In broad terms capital is the amount of funding injected by the business's owners, plus any profits made, less any losses incurred.

Standardised balance sheet format

The layout of a business balance sheet can look rather complex, but in fact it follows what is actually a rather simple mirror-image format to help users of accounts. Once you can see that then any balance sheet becomes much easier to understand.

The symmetry contained within every balance sheet is as follows:

> Long-term assets
> Short-term assets
> ------MIRROR-----
> Short-term liabilities
> Long-term liabilities

Figure 7.2

The long- and short-term element of these categories of assets and liabilities relates to a time horizon 12 months on from the balance sheet date, as follows:

- Long-term assets: these are assets that have an expected use in the business for more than a 12-month period. The more usual name is fixed assets, and examples include buildings, vehicles, plant and equipment.
- Short-term assets: these are assets that would normally be used in the business within the next 12 months. Examples include stocks of raw materials, the value of any jobs-in-progress, stocks of finished product, debtors, funds in the bank.
- Short-term liabilities: these are amounts owed to suppliers of various types, and which fall due for payment

within the next 12 months. Examples include creditors, and bank overdrafts.

- Long-term liabilities: these are amounts owed that fall due for payment after more than 12 months from the balance sheet date. The commonly encountered ones are long-term borrowings due for repayment after 12 months or more, almost invariably long-term finance such as a mortgage.

Balance sheet layouts are standardised in order to allow managers and investors more readily to identify changes in a business's balance sheets from the end of one accounting period to the end of the next one, and to compare the balance sheet strengths of different businesses.

Working capital

Short-term assets and short-term liabilities are adjacent to each other in all balance sheets, and then lumped together to produce a net value of what is known as working capital tied up in the business. Working capital is the amount by which total short-term assets exceeds total short-term liabilities, and is clearly visible in Hedgefrogs Limited's balance sheet below, described using the Companies Act standard label, net current assets.

As noted earlier, a balance sheet also reveals a business's overall net assets position, simply total assets less total liabilities, the amount that a business owes back to its owners.

One confusion factor remains, to do with the jargon. The accounting headings used in the real world differ slightly from the ones noted in Figure 7.2 above, though both the symmetry of layout and the underlying meanings remain precisely the same.

Once you can see the symmetry of the headings above, you will also see that the standard balance sheet headings shown below for Hedgefrogs Limited have the same meanings and are placed in the same relative positions. Note also the standard convention commonly used by accountants to show assets as positive numbers and liabilities as negatives, using brackets to denote the latter.

Hedgefrogs Limited Balance Sheet as at 30 June 200X

	£	£
Fixed assets		22,000
Current assets	46,000	
Current liabilities	(28,000)	
Net current assets (CA – CL)		18,000
Long-term liabilities		(15,000)
Net assets (FA + NCA – LTL)		£ 25,000
Shareholders' funds		£ 25,000

(Shareholder's funds represent share capital, plus profits, less losses, from business commencement to date)

Financial forecasts

The forecasts contained in your business plan represent the direct translation of its narrative script into your expectations for financial performance. In strong business plans these two elements dovetail into each other. The good news is that by the time you start to think about the numbers in detail, you should have analysed your business well enough to translate it into numbers that have credibility. If you have followed the order of chapters in this book, you will have by now analysed your customers' needs, and reviewed your business's offering in the context of rivals and substitutes, and obtained a fix upon the overall potential for sustained profit.

Tip

In order that they fit closely with the narrative sections of your business plan, prepare the financial projections for your business only when you have completed most of the rest of your plan. The numbers are derived from the narrative, it is never the other way around.

To show the importance of the financial section of your business plan, after reading your Executive Summary, most informed readers will turn to the financial forecasts. They will need only a minute or two to scan those and learn a great deal about the quality of the business proposition, and about the competence of the people behind it.

The reasoning for this is that the written word provides flexibility of construction and many fine shades of meaning, but numbers demand precision. If you seek outside funding, the financial forecasts are fundamental, providing interested parties with the ability to assess the financial potential of your business idea.

Tip

Flaws in your business plan's finances will be visible far more readily than defects anywhere else. Financial forecasts are set out in black and white, literally and figuratively, and it is not possible to veil bad news in a way that might just be possible elsewhere in the plan.

When they are credible and well founded, however, the financial projections for your business will communicate the good news quickly to potential investors. They will see the potential returns that your business promises, and understand the funding resources that it needs.

The finance section itself of your plan should present just the headlines, the key financial messages. Most people comprehend visual images more easily than they understand words and numbers. Be aware of this when summarising key financial information, for graphs and bar charts and the use of colour can play a major supporting role in helping you to communicate the figures clearly.

In terms of what to include, detailed financial projections must always be included in your business plan, they are essential. However, there is a risk that if too much detail is presented in the main body of the plan, the messages may become confused. For that reason you should include the detailed forecasts in your plan's appendices.

When using the finance section of your plan to summarise financial highlights, the standard profit and loss account layout shown earlier in this chapter is a good one to use. You should show the forecasts in this summary format for the years covered by your detailed projections. In terms of cashflow, the finance section of your plan should reveal the peak requirements for working capital, and identify the ways in which those requirements will be met. Where forecast balance sheets have been prepared, these too should be provided in the finance section, again in summarised format. Use the standard summary layout shown earlier in this chapter, and seek assistance from a specialist if you need it.

If your business is already trading, your plan's finance section should also highlight recent years' trading results, and the latest balance sheet.

In all cases you should ensure that you cross refer your plan's summarised financials to the detailed figures contained in your plan's appendices, and to the detailed historical business accounts if those are applicable.

Benefits

As well as providing the information needed to determine funding requirements and structure, the business numbers also help on an internal business level. They apply the targets that your business will aim for, and provide the means of measuring progress towards those targets.

In brief, financial forecasts allow the following processes to happen:

- Evaluation of your business's potential by would-be investors and bankers.
- Setting of targets and budgets, so that responsibilities can be handed out and the management of performance delegated.
- Performance measurement against targets, which can themselves be revised based upon actual business results.
- Financial control to be exercised based upon exceptions, so that variances in financial performance beyond acceptable limits are highlighted. That allows management's attention to be directed on the problem areas, the ones that really need attention.

Layouts for financial forecasts

Appendices B and C show specimen layouts for cashflows and forecast profit and loss account, with example figures. This book is not a finance text, but these layouts will provide you with standard formats and headings.

Using spreadsheets to model the finances for your business makes it much easier for you to flex the key variables, such as expected sales volumes, to determine what financial effect these changes would have upon profit levels and upon funding requirements. Predicting the future with 100 per cent accuracy is impossible, and we will return later to the question of 'what if' things are worse, or better, than forecast.

The forecasts in the business plan should show your expectations of what will happen in financial terms, profit and loss and cashflows, on a month-by-month basis for at least the next 24 months. You may decide to include forecasts for a third year as well. There are no fixed rules here, but anything much over even one year is a long way away in business terms, and so it may be not unreasonable to produce the Year 3 profit forecasts on a 'whole year' basis in many cases.

Forecasting for a year as a whole is too long a period, because, for example, a whole year's cash movements will obscure any individual months where large negative cashflows occur.

For instance, it is quite possible for a business to start trading on Day 1 and by the end of (say) Month 5 to have incurred substantial costs, few revenues, and consequent large outflows of cash. The position at the end of Month 5 could be one where a loss had been incurred, and where the cash resources were almost exhausted.

By the end of Month 12, however, the situation for that business might have become somewhat different. If sales started to take off in Month 6, and a positive revenue stream was then generated as a result, cash would start to flow back in from customers. The size of the revenue streams could mean, if things had gone well, that an overall profit was generated by the year-end, with a surplus of liquid funds, cash, building up in the business's bank accounts.

In the above situations, the whole-year position would thus show only the overall profit, and the positive balance of liquid funds by the year end. Yet the month-by-month position on the way towards that year-end would have been very different, with very low funds balances at the end of Month 5.

> **Tip**
>
> Avoid hidden dips. By forecasting on a month-by-month basis any otherwise hidden dips in cash balances will become visible, and will allow you to see the levels of funding resources needed in each individual month in order to allow your business to trade successfully through its cash-negative stages.

As a result of their shape when plotted as a graph, the movements of liquid funds for a new business are sometimes known as the Death Valley curve. The aim, of course, is that after an initial steep descent in its cash balances, however, a new business may begin to generate revenue streams and haul itself out of the descent. The Death Valley imagery is all about having sufficient resources available to be able to survive.

On a more positive note, the shape of that curve for businesses that eventually succeed will resemble a tick symbol when plotted graphically. Over time, cash balances generated by the business continue to climb and the curve assumes a tick shape.

Assumptions must be stated

It is important to inform readers of your business plan about the assumptions that underlie the financial forecasts, so that they can review these for reasonableness. If, for example, you expect that your business's customers will, on average, pay your business for their purchases within two months, 60 days, then state that assumption clearly. If you anticipate that your business will pay its own suppliers after 30 days, on average, explain that assumption.

> **Tip**
>
> Explain all key assumptions that have been made when preparing the financial forecasts. Other examples will include, for example, the numbers of employees required and when they will be recruited, business space requirements, and the growth in sales volumes anticipated over time.

Sales forecasting

> **Tip**
>
> Predicting future sales revenues requires particular care. It is never easy, although some types of business lend themselves more readily to the forecasting potential demand than others.

A retail fashion business, for example, should be able to gather data about the passing footfall on the pavement outside. By possessing a clear understanding of how its potential market was made up, in demographic terms, age and gender, for example, that business could then make estimates about the numbers of passers-by who were potential customers, in their own right and on behalf of others. Those estimates could then be translated into figures by making credible assumptions about average spending levels per customer.

For all businesses, it might be possible to look at competitors' sales performance figures, and then relate those to the business's situation, obtaining the information needed from business libraries perhaps, and other credible sources on the internet. Note that sources of market data should always be verified, and stated clearly in your plan.

Businesses that are already trading will have some sales history to use as a starting point for producing sales forecasts. For a new business, however, estimates will need to be made of when it is expected that the revenue stream, the first sales, will be made.

Tip

The volume, timing, and expected growth rate of sales revenues are all very difficult to predict accurately. To get around this problem, one useful approach is to prepare a set of forecasts that show your best estimate of what will happen, the expected case, the sales outcome you think most likely, and then to prepare another set showing what you believe will be the worst position. Producing two sets of forecasts, expected case and worst case, will help to ensure that your own belief in the business does not lead you only to produce overly-optimistic forecasts of future sales revenues.

It is also possible to estimate expected sales by using some very simple probability theory. After deciding, with due caution, the month in which sales will first occur, your next task is to predict a likely range of sales values. You can estimate both the best case and worst case sales forecasts by reviewing the factors that will determine whether customers purchase, and in what quantities.

Both Porter's Five Forces model and the PEST analysis that you have already performed for your business can provide very useful data at this point. Remind yourself about the expected strength of your business in profit terms and about the external factors that impact directly upon demand. Remember that seasonality factors affect many businesses, as do fashions and trends. Many businesses find that sales performance is strongly linked to the weather, so ponder carefully all factors that will impact upon your business.

The best and worst case sales estimates for your business plan will incorporate whatever relevant and credible information you are able to derive. The next step is to forecast expected sales figures using subjectively assessed probabilities. If using broad brush probabilities in this way sounds rather like guesswork, it is at least informed guesswork. As such it will be much better as a forecasting method than the figures conjured out of nowhere that are found in many business plans. The example below shows how it all fits together.

After considering all of the information available to you, you estimate the next month's potential sales figures to be as follows:

- Best case £25,000
- Worst case £15,000

The next step is to decide upon the percentage likelihood of each case. You decide that there is one chance in five of achieving the best case sales figure, a 50 per cent chance of achieving a sales figure half way between the two, and a 30 per cent chance of achieving worst case sales.

Those estimates can be used to let you establish an expected value for sales, as follows:

£ ((20% x 25,000) + (50% x ((25,000+15,000) / 2))
+ (30% x 15,000))
= £ (5,000 + 10,000 + 4,500)
= £19,500

As noted above, this method is neither objective nor scientific despite the usage of percentages, since both the sales values and the percentages applied to them are personal estimates, made on a subjective basis. Nevertheless, the £19,500 expected value figure accommodates weighted-by-probability best-case and worst-case positions. If all months are forecast using this technique, the overall result can turn out to be remarkably accurate. Repeating the expected value process across a number of months can produce more credible estimates, which means more realistic and more readily justified sales revenue forecasts.

If you decide to use this expected value approach to sales forecasting, it is still worth preparing a worst-case set of figures. That will give you a reality check, an indication of what the business's financial position will be if only the lowest sales figure is actually achieved.

Tip

However you produce the sales forecasts for your business, always stand back when they are completed. Ask yourself honestly how you would see those same figures if another person had given them to you for your comment. Would you really think that they were achievable?

A method too often encountered in business plans is one in which a round-sum percentage sales growth factor is built into the financial forecast spreadsheets, and the effects of the compounding becomes visible in the steeply rising sales revenues line. Round-sum percentage increases are almost certainly too simplistic, their effects are too easily visible, and as a result perfectly sound business plans can be contain a pervasive sense of financial unreality.

Forecasting costs

It is also possible to use an estimated value method when forecasting business expenditure, but you may find that this is not necessary. As we have seen, business costs can be divided in broad terms into those that are fixed, and those that are variable.

Future levels of business fixed costs, overheads, are generally rather easier to predict than are sales revenues. The first step is to determine what types of fixed costs your business will be likely to incur. It may be helpful to use the cost headings set out in Appendix D as a guide to the categories of costs that may be relevant. Planning your business's resource requirements will enable you to establish the likely level of future fixed costs quite accurately.

The accuracy of your forecasts of variable costs, however, must depend upon the accuracy of your sales forecasts. By definition, variable costs vary with the amount of sales; they are directly linked to sales. It follows that any overestimates or underestimates in sales forecasts, whether in amounts or timing, will produce directly consequential inaccuracies in costs.

For established businesses, the position is generally slightly easier, since a cost history will be available. The challenge in that situation lies in considering carefully the effects of forecast changes in sales volumes. Are these accurately mirrored by forecast changes to a business's costs structure, higher sales leading to larger premises requirements, and greater administration staff numbers, for example?

Financing growth

Rapid growth in sales would appear a good thing, and in many respects it is, of course. It also brings pressures at many levels, however, and has a major potential downside. Business growth usually has negative cashflow implications, since growing businesses swallow cash.

This fact is not always anticipated. A rapidly growing business needs to have access to more and more working capital, simply to fund the growing cashflow time-lag, to be able pay the ever-increasing amounts of liabilities to suppliers before the higher revenues flow back in its bank account. If growth continues, this problem is not resolved even when cash does flow back in again, of course, since ever-growing cash outflows to suppliers will always precede subsequent funds inflows from customers.

Businesses can and do run out of cash if they expand more quickly than predicted. Salvation lies in preparing carefully considered cashflow forecasts, so that this trap for the unwary can be foreseen, and planned for by arranging additional bank overdraft facilities, for example. Another possibility is to obtain one of the many forms of invoice discounting facility that are available, essentially funding methods by which a third party finance company purchases a business's sales invoices at a discount, thus making funds available more quickly to that business but at the expense of the finance charge that the discount represents.

> ### Tip
> Careful forward planning is needed to accommodate rapid sales growth. There exists a big risk that fast-growing businesses start to 'overtrade', which means that their available working capital becomes insufficient to cope with the greater demands placed upon it as amounts of liquid funds held up in the cashflow time-lag increase.

Conclusion

In many cases business plans are required to play a pivotal role in raising the finance needed to start a business, or to allow one to expand. Getting the financial parts of your plan right is essential, and a poorly prepared financial section will blight the credibility of an otherwise strong business plan.

In any event, having a firm grip on the financial situation is essential for all businesses. Business financial statements, the accounts, play a vital supporting role to management, providing raw data from which business information can be extracted and based on which business decisions can be made.

Conventional business accounts have a few limitations, they do not measure broader environmental costs very well, nor do they really measure what might be called social costs. Many non-accountants are surprised to discover that underneath the surface business accounting is sometimes art as much as science. Despite its focus upon figures, finance is underpinned by subjective judgements and assumptions, driven by experience and, on occasions, by gut-feel. That does not invalidate them; it simply reflects the reality that being in business is about making judgements on so many levels, finance included.

Getting to grips with business finance requires the acquisition of some basic knowledge, and requires that you provide yourself with access to accountants who can explain things clearly without resorting to jargon. It is the obligation of accountants to explain accounts to non-accountants, demystifying them in order to make them understandable.

The points below are the ones to hold on to firmly when dealing with accountants:

- Accounts are never an end in themselves, though their role is vital one in supporting sound business decisions.
- The concept of cashflow is more important than the concept of profit, and fortunately the timing of cashflows can be managed and improved. Cash now is better than cash later.
- Businesses fail when they run out of cash, which can happen even when they are trading profitably.
- Make sure that you understand the difference between gross profit and net profit and understand the contribution principle explained above.
- If accounts fail to communicate their messages clearly then they are pointless.

Tip

Never allow yourself to be put off by the jargon, nor by accountants who do not translate financial information into plain English. Accounts are about communicating fundamentally important financial information about businesses, and if the communication process breaks down then accounts lose their purpose.

A profit and loss account gathers together, for a defined period, total revenues generated, the sales figure, and the costs incurred in earning that revenue. Deducting those costs from revenues earned reveals whether an overall profit has been created, or whether a loss has been incurred.

A balance sheet sets out a business's assets and its liabilities all at a fixed point. The cashflow statement links the balance sheet to the profit and loss account, since it shows how streams of revenues and costs result in actual movements of cash.

Standard accounts reporting formats exist, but be aware that these are often modified by accountants to fit a particular business's circumstances more precisely. The roots of all layouts used will be traceable back to the basic model, however, the form and content of accounts set out in this chapter. If financial statements that you see do not appear to fit the standard, always ask the person who prepared them to explain the layout and what it shows. Be fearless in this. If you do not understand, ask and ask again until you do understand.

The process of forecasting future financial performance is a subjective process requiring estimates, sometimes guesstimates. It is almost never an exact science. However, by careful analysis of the information that is available, forecasts can be made that will if necessary stand up to the detailed scrutiny of potential investors and funders.

Finally, forecasts also serve to provide a business with a measuring device, and targets to strive towards. They project the business's future in financial terms, and in doing so show the rewards that are potentially available, the financial returns potentially achievable by investors. Forecasts must always be credible, but since the real world is a place where events do not always go according to plan, without a crystal ball it is impossible to predict the future with unfailing accuracy.

INSTANT TIP

If you aren't sure about something, ask. Arm yourself with a competent accountant who can and will explain things. Then ask again until you are sure.

08

Appendices and supporting information: how do I include everything without including absolutely everything?

Introduction

The last part of your business plan contains the appendices. There exist a number of business areas where supporting documents and background information are needed to assist the reader's understanding of the business.

The appendices let you place necessary, but detailed, information at the end of the plan. It is there available for reference, but does not clog up the efficient flow of the rest of the plan.

Typical contents

Appendixes to business plans typically contain the following types of detailed information:

- **CVs of the key individuals connected with the business**
  These will, of course, provide detailed insights into the backgrounds, qualifications, and experience of the people who are responsible for delivering the plan. It helps readers if all CVs adopt a reasonably consistent format.

- **Organisation structure**

- **Technical back-up information**   Your plan itself should talk to its audience in a way that an informed lay person can understand. In many situations, the more complex technical details may be needed as back-up and for reference, and an appendix is the correct place for that.

- **Detailed financial information**   The financial section of your plan should present the business's key financial data in summarised form, highlighting the big issues in financial terms and spelling out the key financial elements of the plan. Detailed financial forecasts are essential as back-up, put them in an appendix. Provide readers with detailed forecasts, and details also of the assumptions under which they have been prepared. If your business is already trading, then summarised key information from the historical accounts will also be useful to readers.

- **Detailed SWOT and PEST analyses**

- **Other documents, depending upon individual circumstances**   More common ones include detailed market research results, expressions of interest from potential customers, information about competitors' businesses, any intellectual property rights registrations, such as patents, details of other intangible assets, including brand and trade names, copies of major contracts, and other important legal documents where these would help a reader's understanding of a particular issue.

Conclusion

Keep your business plan focused. Detailed information must be included in the appendixes only if is directly relevant, which means that it adds something substantial to readers' understanding of your business. Including sales brochures and proposed advertisements might be relevant, for example, but only if these provide readers with information that backed up the marketing section of your business plan.

The only generalisation is that you should use your own judgement. Just like the rest of your business plan, the contents of the appendices reflect back on you. Quantity is never the same thing as quality, and the appendices are not a general repository for any other information that might just be relevant. If they do deteriorate into a catch-all filing system, then readers may associate that with some muddled thinking.

INSTANT TIP

Keep your business plan focussed. Detailed information must be included in the appendices only if directly relevant, which means that it adds something substantial to readers' understanding of your business.

09

Raising the funds: how do I raise the finance needed, and how do I decide who should get what?

Man who stand on hill with mouth wide open wait long time for roast duck to drop in.

Chinese proverb

Introduction

The main structure of your business plan is now complete. This chapter provides an overview of funding issues, since so many business plans have within their remit the need to secure financial resources.

In situations where securing financial backing is one of your short-term priorities, then a compelling business plan becomes the key to open locked doors. Unless you can obtain the finance needed, in the right form, and have it available over the right timescale, then your business will not happen in the first place, or it will not be able to continue trading.

As is so often the case in business, it is determination that is the essential personal attribute. Approaching would-be financial backers is like approaching potential customers – you may have to move far outside your personal comfort zone and face rejection. It is highly unlikely that funders will come to you. You may indeed experience rejection, quite possibly several times, but the trick lies in *not giving up*.

Types of funding

If a business requires funding then it needs funders to provide the cash, cash that can arrive in a number of ways:

- Long-term share capital.
- Long-term borrowings.
- Short-term overdraft facilities from a bank.
- Short-term finance from other sources, mainly funds raised from invoice discounting facilities, as noted in the previous chapter.
- Internal finance facilities.

Tip

Whatever type or types of funding are required in your business's particular circumstances, there is only one correct approach to obtaining it. That is to prepare your plan as a plan for the business, and to show the business's funding requirements as an integral part of that.

A business's funding requirements arise out of its business needs, therefore. No matter how difficult the process of securing financial backing, as long as your business proposition is sound, and as long as your business plan is prepared thoroughly, and as long as you are determined enough, you will be able to secure the funding needed. The route may be not at all the one that you anticipated, or only partially, but if you are competent and if your business is sound, a route there will be.

Sources of long-term finance

Remember your elevator pitch, your verbally polished and rehearsed Executive Summary. You may end up delivering that pitch a half a dozen times or more when your plan has succeeded just enough for you to be telephoned for an initial chat, or for you to have been invited to an informal and preliminary meeting. Somehow, somewhere in those pitches, wheels within wheels, you may find a door of opportunity opening a fraction, just enough for you to insert a metaphorical foot.

The door may be that to one of the numerous venture capital funds, many of which specialise in certain business areas. These VCs, as they are known, have as one of their own primary business needs the identification of suitable investment opportunities. Or the door might lead to someone located via one of the various Business Angel networks, whose function is to link businesses that require relatively small amounts of funding with entrepreneurial individuals who have funds available and a wish to invest.

Typically, Business Angels invest sums between around £25,000 and £250,000. Those individuals are often successful entrepreneurs themselves, and they may be willing and able to bring their skills and experience to your venture. In the UK, in fact, there exist special tax breaks to encourage them to do so.

What investment means

Anyone who invests in a business in return for some of the share capital, equity as it is often called, is taking a slice of the ownership for themselves. They are investing in what is, to a greater or lesser extent, a risky business venture.

Share capital may also be available from tamer targets, your personal contacts, mainly friends and relatives, as well as from outside investors. The latter will almost certainly be more demanding, and seek more for their money. That is more ownership, more control, greater safeguards.

The hardest place to obtain funding is from outsiders, especially if your business is at start-up, just about to begin trading activities, or very near to that point. Your business will be, by definition, at an early stage, largely unproven, and very high risk.

Tip

Always build your business as far as you are able using your own resources. That in itself will demonstrate your determination and commitment in taking things as far as you can on your own.

Levels of risk

At and around the start-up stage, much can still go wrong, and the most risky situation of all is for funding that is needed by a business at what is known as the seed capital stage, for the development of an as yet unproven concept. That business concept may never come to fruition at all, never even get to the starting line, especially when significant development stages remain outstanding. What funders much prefer to see is proof of concept at least, certainty that a new idea will actually work.

Often directly connected to that, timescales for market readiness often slip, allowing competitors to catch up or even to reach target customers first, picking off the easy wins, the low-hanging fruit. Not least, would-be funders are fully aware that in many cases costs may, which means will, be higher than expected.

Once a business has started trading, however, and particularly when initial sales have already been made, or firm orders placed at least, then the levels of perceived and actual risk fall for the outside investor. Investors' own needs are about maximising the likelihood of their potential upside, their future financial gains, and minimising the size of the risks they face. From this it follows that so-called development capital, essentially funding for the further development of, growth of, a tried and tested business, is easier to obtain. Providing development capital is a much less risky activity for investors than providing risk capital for brand new ideas.

If you take a step back to look at the whole picture, you will see that the degree of risk that various business funding situations represent can be graded. A risk profile running from low to high is as follows:

- Existing proven profitable business seeking funds for further expansion.
- Internal management team taking over existing business from outgoing owners (MBO: Management Buy Out).
- External management team taking over existing business (MBI: Management Buy In).
- Refinance for a business financial rescue where previous problems are clearly understood and reasonable.
- Business start-ups.
- Seed capital where the funding is for the development of an unproven business concept.

Outside investors come in many shapes and sizes, the fundamental approach that they share is about reducing their risks to a minimum. Many specialise in specific sectors or in certain types of technology. They will minimise their risk by investing across a spread of different businesses, some of which will fail, most may end up going nowhere, but a handful are expected to hit a large enough jackpot to produce a substantial return overall for the investors. Other VC funds spread their risk by investing across different industry sectors, thus sidestepping higher risk levels that can exist when everything is concentrated within one business area – too many eggs in one basket.

Persuading investors

Your business plan has to convince the people that you need to convince of the following:

- That the type of business, the industry, and its marketplace, its target customers, represent an attractive business proposition. Think of Porter's Five Forces model and your PEST analysis.
- That your business's product or service is special, which means that it can be differentiated readily from the offerings of direct competitors, and from substitute products and services. Your business plan must explain the key features that provide a significant advantage in customers' eyes, that they are willing to pay for.
- That it is not easy for others to copy your business's special features, and that high entry barriers are in place to encourage potential new entrants to go elsewhere.
- That your business's product or service has future growth; what is often referred to as scalability. It must possess attributes that meet the needs of the largest number of potential buyers, not just the needs of a small niche.
- That your financial model is realistic. Profit and loss forecasts and the projected cashflow profile must be robust able to withstand detailed scrutiny and compelling which means showing attractive potential returns.

- That the management team possesses the personal attributes and the business skills to be able to deliver the business plan. These include technical skills, welded to grit and an utter determination to succeed, plus a degree of financial commitment to the success of the business.

Sources of short-term finance

The task of obtaining a suitable working capital facility, funding needed to cover the cashflow cycle, from a business's clearing bank may be more straightforward. This is particularly true if assets of easily realisable worth, owned by your business, or by you, or others, are available for the bank to use as security.

Banks generally expect to place a legal charge over assets pledged as security for loans. A charge is a legal device, granted by a borrower to a lender, which ensures that if the borrower defaults on a loan, the lender has the power to seize the assets held under the charge and sell them so that the loan can be repaid. Unlike venture capital funds and Business Angels, high street clearing banks are not in the risk-lending business, they make advances of other people's money, their depositors' monies, on a low-risk basis by providing finance facilities that are secured against assets.

The basic workings of invoice discounting facilities were outlined briefly in the preceding chapter. You should note that the finance companies providing these types of funding facilities will expect to take a legal charge over a business's debtors, so that they too have a safety net beneath them if things go wrong.

Internal corporate funding

Securing internal company funding may be simple or rather complex, depending upon the particular business and the procedures that accompany it. The hoops to be jumped through may be large and near to the ground, or small and rather high. It all depends upon the particular situation.

> **Tip**
>
> In any event, however, and as is the case for all potential funders, a strong business plan, one that makes the business case clearly, has a much better chance of attracting the funding required than a weak one. Where a number of projects exist, or in situations where several departments are all competing in a bidding process for limited funds, then the metaphor once more is the one about putting on your metaphorical running shoes and making sure that you can out-run your rivals.

Sharing the risks and rewards of business ownership

The ownership of limited companies is defined by the holding of shares in those companies. To obtain external equity funding, you will need to give up shares. Many people are not comfortable with that idea initially, but the funds made available to your business, and the additional business expertise that may then be on tap, are both designed to make the size of the overall business cake larger of course.

A reassuring factor exists when negotiating with potential external funders. Although their need is to maximise the potential returns from their investment, and to minimise the risks, they will be conscious that if they are too greedy then your goose may never lay its golden eggs. Professional investors know that a business's founders will only put in the management effort and commitment needed to achieve success if they also stand to obtain a significant slice of the potential rewards. It hardly needs saying that if members of the key management team lose their incentive and motivation, then a business run by those people is very unlikely to succeed.

Outside investors have to obtain enough ownership to provide them with a level of potential reward that matches their risk. Managers have to hold on to or be able to obtain via share options enough ownership to ensure that they remain sufficiently incentivised to perform. Put simply, share options are contracts that allow shares to be purchased, usually on very favourable terms, as long as specified key business performance targets are met.

Two areas are critical in getting the right balance, sharing the risks and rewards in a way that is perceived as fair by both sides. The first is about how investors go about valuing business opportunities, the second is about understanding what varying percentage ownership stakes mean in terms of the degrees of control they give outside investors.

What is my business worth?

'How much is my business worth?' is a question frequently asked. The answer is frustrating: it is worth what a willing purchaser is prepared to pay, and different purchasers will be willing to pay different amounts. In other words, there is no easy valuation method for most businesses. The purchaser who will pay the most is likely to be the one with the greatest need, whose business has a gap into which yours fits. A good purchaser is one who believes that they can to add value to your business and that your business will add value to theirs.

Financial and statistical techniques that are employed to establish business valuations by would-be purchasers, and indeed would-be investors, are outlined below. However, if you think of your business as a large and unique detached house then you will see more easily that although a broad assessment of its value can be made, a range, the exact price will depend in the end upon what a willing buyer is prepared to pay. Accurate assessments of the value of almost identical smaller houses in an estate setting can be made by looking at recent sales prices, each house providing the benchmark value for others. Unique houses, however, do not have such easily available comparators, only broad indicators.

The price of such a house will hinge upon factors such as desirability of location, its size and that of its plot, whether there is potential for further development, internal layout, quality of construction and internal fittings, state of internal decoration, state of the housing market itself, and so on. It will also depend upon how many potential buyers want it. Two or more proceedable purchasers who each badly want the same property will bid against each other and drive the price up.

So it is with a business. The intrinsic value of a business, usually measured by its expected future profit stream, has a major impact in determining worth. A business's external potential will link to that, its fit with other businesses. Where more than one interested investor or purchaser exists, a business's value will be a function of how keen each potential investor or purchaser is to acquire a stake, or indeed the whole business. Degree of keenness is determined by how much profit potential is expected.

Just as for a house, it is certainly possible to maximise the price achievable for a successful business by preparing it for a future sale. At one level are cosmetic factors that can be addressed. Paying dividends to reduce salary costs, for example, will have a cosmetic impact upon the appearance of a business's profit and loss account. At a deeper level there are many areas in which taking action sooner rather than later can make a business more saleable. Resolving any potentially messy legal issues that may hang over the business, making yourself uncritical to the business, and locking in key managers by various means, for example.

Measuring financial returns

Mathematical techniques known as Discounted Cash Flow (DCF) and its sibling, the Internal Rate of Return (IRR), are used by funders and financiers to establish now, in the present, the value of future financial returns available from potential investments. These techniques rely on the financial predictions made for investment opportunities, the business financial forecasts, to calculate expected future returns.

Tip

From the viewpoint of your own business plan, it is sufficient to know that the techniques outlined below exist, so that when the terminology is used you are familiar with the basic principles. Your plan is your focus. Make sure that your plan's financial forecasts are credible and let others work out what the level of return is for them.

In broad terms, DCF uses future returns as measured by the cash generated by a business, and re-calculates these in the context of their expected timescales in order to calculate a return now, a net present value, NPV, of those future returns. To do this, a so-called discount rate is used, a target percentage rate of return that the investor aims for.

IRR is another way of looking at future returns, but instead of bringing future cashflows back to a net present value, it takes expected the future profit returns and re-calculates these as a percentage rate of return figure. IRR is the rate of return that brings the present value of future cashflows equal to the initial outlay, the cost of the investment.

The IRR technique allows potential investors to compare an expected return with their own internal required rate of return from investments. This may be referred to as a 'hurdle' rate of return, in that investors will consider only potential investment opportunities that are predicted to produce a level of profit that exceeds, clears, the required hurdle rate. By taking only those investment opportunities that exceed a required minimum rate, an investor should be able, over time, to build a portfolio of business investments that generate a long-run return of at least that required level.

What various shareholding stakes represent

Understanding what various fractions of company ownership really mean is an important issue. How much of your business should you be prepared to give up, and what would that loss of ownership mean to you?

Some people's aim is to build their business and retain control of it, control being the critical word. Holding shares in a limited company usually gives the owner a right to vote on major company issues at meetings of shareholders. The broad position under UK companies' legislation is that any individual shareholder, or group of individuals, who control more than 50 per cent of the ordinary voting shares in a company will have a controlling stake.

Legal agreements can exist within individual companies to vary the situation, but the general principle is that more than 50 per cent voting power equates to control for most purposes. That is because a greater than 50 per cent majority has the voting power to approve ordinary resolutions, ones that require only a simple, meaning greater than 50 per cent, majority in order to be passed.

Such resolutions would normally comprise decisions about the appointment of someone as company director, which firm of accountants will be appointed as the company's auditors, if applicable, and whether there should be a dividend payable to shareholders.

Complete control is self-evidently in the hands of any individual or group that votes 100 per cent of the voting shares in a company.

In reality, however, any individual or group that holds 75 per cent of a company's voting shares virtually possesses complete control, since they have the power to approve so-called special resolutions, and extraordinary resolutions. Those are the types of resolutions that require 75 per cent of the voting shareholders' approval, such as changing a company's name or deciding to wind it up.

Non-voting shares

If you fall into that group of people who do not wish to relinquish control, then if your business requires funding you might aim for softer target funders, namely friends and family. You might decide to issue them with shares in the company, but shares of a different type that do not give holders any right to vote on company resolutions. Various kinds of non-voting shares exist, and many potential ownership structures are possible. Having laterally-thinking and creative professional advisers to hand is essential in this area.

Non-voting shares will still benefit from any increase in the value of the business as a whole as it grows. However, since such shares do not confer a vote to the holders, family and friends shareholders do not have the chance, as the founder may see things, of becoming too closely involved in determining business matters.

Investment process

Where outside equity investment is involved, the investment process is a complex one of detailed negotiations between the parties. That means having a shrewd head for negotiations as much as possessing keen financial skills. Decisions about shares and funding structures sit right at the heart of things, they are pivotal, and are not areas in which to cut corners.

Always draw on the services of competent professional advisers to guide you about what fraction of your business to give up in exchange for what amount of equity, share capital, and the many dozens of related issues that will need to be addressed and resolved.

Conclusion

Investors assess risk. Businesses that are at or around start-up are high-risk propositions, and when the funding need is for seedcorn capital, developing a business that is really only at the concept stage, the risks of failure are very high. The reality is that seedcorn capital is extraordinarily difficult to obtain.

In any event, securing the funding that your business needs will always be made easier if a strong business case exists, contained within a compelling business plan, both narrative and numbers. There are no fixed rules for the availability of funding, however, since so much depends upon the specific circumstances of each deal and upon the degree of determination of the individuals seeking backing for their business.

All potential funding sources aim to reduce their risk levels to an acceptable minimum. It follows that funders who specialise in certain sectors, biotechnology or leisure or telecommunications, for example, will have particular understanding of those types of businesses and the risk levels that they represent. They may thus be willing to contemplate a higher level of risk for a given project than more general investment funds.

Investment in equity, share ownership, is always a fundamentally high-risk investment activity nonetheless. If you have the ability to access family-and-friends sources of finance, you will find that their approach can be in many respects a less demanding one than that of outside professional investors. Other issues may then arise, however, lack of objectivity being a potential big one.

Beyond establishing that your business funding need fits within a business sector and a risk profile that a funder is willing to contemplate, these are the boxes that professional venture capital investors will want to tick:

- Share ownership fraction that gives them a significant slice of future business success.
- Suitably experience and balanced management team.
- Clear management commitment to the business.
- Clear differentiation from rivals' products or services.
- High entry barriers.
- Strong financial prospects.
- Door marked 'exit' visible somewhere in the middle distance, certainly well within five years or so.

From your end of things, ensure that you understand the degrees of control provided by various percentage shareholding stakes. Professional help and guidance is essential in this area, so locate plain-speaking advisers. The question of what size of stake in your business you should give up in return for the funding that your business needs is the Very Big Question in terms of its long-term consequences.

INSTANT TIP

Whatever types of funding are required in your business's particular circumstances, there is only one correct approach to obtaining it. That is to prepare your plan as a plan for the business and to show the business's funding requirements as an integral part of that.

10

How do I avoid the most common business plan pitfalls?

The biggest danger of all is often not the hidden one, it is the one in full view that you cannot see.

Introduction

The issues set out here need no introduction, each one has been covered in this book. Work through the bullet points below, use them as a checklist for ensuring that your plan does not commit any of the major blunders.

In business the right things will happen if you are determined to make them happen. In exactly the same way, most pitfalls can be avoided if you can make yourself aware of them and are determined to avoid them.

Objectivity

Above everything keep on asking yourself what you would think if someone else had handed you your plan for comments. Be ruthlessly honest with yourself before others do that for you.

Pitfalls

- Not stating the purpose of your plan.
- Making grandiose claims that say nothing: 'ABC Blocks aims to be the best supplier of recycled glass blocks in the UK.' What does 'best' mean? Objectives must be:
  - Specific;
  - Measurable;
  - Achievable;
  - Realistic (do-able within the resources available);
  - Time-targeted.
- Making generalisations and unsupported statements of fact. If your plan relies on statistics about the potential customers and the industry, quote sources and check that they are credible.
- Form over substance. Slick presentation is fine, but not if it papers over cracks in the content in an attempt to conceal weaknesses. There is no such thing as a perfect plan, a perfect entrepreneur, or a perfect business. Acknowledge any major negative issues that exist and say how you will resolve them.
- Unrelenting optimism about sales volumes. Does your business concept really have scalability, or is it destined to remain relatively small?
- 'We need only one per cent' syndrome – a hope that a large potential market will automatically equate to being able to secure a small slice of that market. Your plan

needs credible sales forecasts that will stand up to independent scrutiny and verification. Do the legwork.

- Underestimating costs and underestimating timescales.
- Claiming that any idea is risk free. It isn't.
- An apparent absence of competition, or very little. Rivals almost certainly exist, but you have missed them. If they are not direct rivals, they may be copycat offerings with marginal differences, potential competitors lurking in the wings, or substitutes on which customers can choose to spend their money.
- Marketing strategies that name everything you can think of: 'Our marketing effort relies on advertising, viral marketing, PR, point of sale material, product placement, the internet, recruiting a highly experienced marketing director, telemarketing, and a network of independent sales agents.'
- Your business plan must be logical and linear. Plans that are too long and present things in a meandering way do not suggest clarity of thinking. Beginning. Muddle. End. Avoid.
- Lapsing into jargon. Non-specialists must be able to understand your plan. As an aside, know that not all, but very many people draw negative conclusions from poor spelling and punctuation. Use spelling and grammar checkers, there is no excuse for being lazy.
- Omitting a reality check. Perform the sort of reality check that can kick in at 3 a.m. even for the most optimistic individuals. Do not do it at 3 a.m., however.
- Not focusing in on the key numbers. Do not build acres of spreadsheets that include predictions of your business's likely expenditure on teaspoons in three years' time.
- Grit and commitment not evident in the plan, nor indeed in the way that things have developed so far.
- Not addressing possible legal complications. Does anyone else have a share of the proprietorial interest in your product or service? Is there a risk of claims that you have taken someone else's designs or ideas?

What happens next

Completing your business plan is actually a beginning in itself of course. Your business's success will come out of the many decisions that follow: big ones and small ones, sometimes wrong but the majority right, made day after day, week after week. The secret of success is being able to pile good decisions upon good decisions as the business progresses towards its desired objectives.

You will maximise your business's chances of business success, of getting those decision right, if you continually keep your business plan under review. Successful businesses keep fine-tuning all aspects of their activities to do better what they do that meets customers' needs. Those needs change and evolve over time, and that means keeping them clearly in view, together with your competitors' own responses to them.

Focus always on what your customers want, not what you have, and keep innovating in order to keep ahead, to run faster than your competitors. That approach enshrines the fundamental attitude for success in business life, a way of being, a mindset to possess.

Research and management theory contribute an enormously valuable academic discipline to business, but successful businesses are always be underpinned also by native wit and resource as well, and by individuals' sheer determination to succeed. The real world never exactly fits any business model, because it contains far too many of humanity's glorious imperfections.

You will make things happen if you are determined enough to make things happen, and the payback for business success is high, well beyond any financial reward. The adrenalin buzz from succeeding becomes addictive for some, as does others' recognition for what an entrepreneur has achieved. Your task is to make sure that you are not so busy building the business that you find yourself bogged down all the time, buried by operational detail.

Tip

Force time into your diary, shoehorn in a couple of hours each month in which you can escape from the tyranny of telephone, email and the fax machine. Review and update your business plan, let your plan be the catalyst that produces that business luxury, time for reflection, time to think.

The End

At which point this book ends. Some people evolve into compulsive entrepreneurs, needing their regular fix. They obtain their kicks from taking on big challenges, from solving problems creatively, from out-running the competition, from peer recognition, and from making money too, as a by-product. In running any business, the risks, the problems, the hours, and the potential rewards are different from those of individuals who occupy their days with more regular jobs.

The UK's business culture has never been more entrepreneurial than in recent times, certainly not since the undiluted market economics of the Victorian era and all preceding aeons. For those who choose to pursue the challenge of building their own business, on their own account or with others, the enjoyment of doing it and the likelihood of business success are both greatly improved by devising a strong, workable business plan, and then implementing it.

The Grizzly Bear story appeared at the start of this book and will end it. As has been said before you do not have an absolutely perfect business model, excellent though yours may be, nor a completely unflawed idea, nor a completely unchallengeable product or service. You may be a world-class manager, whatever that means, but you will never be perfect. In the real world, your task, you business's task, is to supply the needs of the people that you want as customers by simply being better than the opposition. That is nearly always possible if you are determined enough.

Reflect upon the last paragraph. From that perspective your task is rather less daunting.

So, think for yourself, do your homework, put in the hours and produce a professional and compelling business plan. You will end up producing a document that is quite simply better than most other business plans, fact.

Good luck!

INSTANT TIP

Force time into your diary, shoehorn a couple of hours each month in which you can escape from the tyranny of telephone, email, and fax machine. Review and update your business plan and let it be the catalyst that produces that business luxury, time to think.

Appendices

Appendix A: Example SWOT analysis: Gloopy Cookie Company

Gloopy Cookie Company

STRENGTHS

strong image/profile/contacts
A & B very different personalities
product fun image and reputation
memorable
USP name IPR protected
well-known
product name becoming generic name
self-service avoid queues
brand awareness & profile
unique recipes
product knowledge
staff team enthusiasm
loyalty
ideas generation
PR team top in sector
website growth: 50% (was 30% last year)
high organic and environmental image ratings
two pilot franchise outlets already successfully trading

WEAKNESSES

disorganization/office can be chaotic
decisions can be too spontaneous/impulsive
lack of planning
last minute
financial confidence
product costings
too much choice for customers?
absence of direction
day-to-day firefighting rather than strategy
information systems outgrown
insufficient capital to roll out franchise model

OPPORTUNITIES

customer list/8k names on mailing list
database mining
complementary product ranges
price fine tuning
supply chain management cost down via competitive tenders
keep streamline product range to best-selling flavours
better sourcing of ingredients
potential investors hovering
trade sale to complementary business
royal warrant on horizon 3 more years to go out of 5
building high street property portfolio
point of sale product ranges, gift market, 'gloopy-time' crockery
spin-off merchandising
athletic sponsorships

THREATS

Droopy Cookies continue to compete on cost
DC unpredictable/nuisance value
other copycats in future
inadequate focus on finance/cashflow
key staff leaving
economic cycle changes lower customer leisure spend
family tensions between A & B post divorce

Appendix B: Example cashflow forecast: Enkryptikon Limited

ENKRYPTIKON LIMITED BEST/WORST/EXPECTED CASE ...

List of assumptions ....

Cashflow projections for the twelve month period ending 28 February 2011

	2010										2011		Total
	March £	April £	May £	June £	July £	Aug £	Sept £	Oct £	Nov £	Dec £	Jan £	Feb £	£
CASH INFLOW:													
Receipts from customers >	0	0	0	0	0	0	0	0	0	0	0	88,125	88,125
Equity funding: founders	5,000												5,000
Equity funding: VC			175,000										175,000
Interest received					1000			750			400		2,150
TOTAL RECEIPTS	5,000	0	175,000	0	1,000	0	0	750	0	0	400	88,125	270,275
CASH OUTFLOW:													
Components >													
Other materials >													
Salaries			10,000	10,000	10,000	12,000	12,000	12,000	12,000	16,000	16,000	16,000	126,000
Employer's NIC			1,280	1,280	1,280	1,536	1,536	1,536	1,536	2,048	2,048		14,080
Rent			3,000			3,000			3,000			3,000	12,000
Rates and water		300	300	300	300	300	300	300	300	300	300		3,000
Light, heat and power >					353			353			353		1,059
Administration salaries		500	500	500	500	500	500	500	500	500	500		5,000

ENKRYPTIKON LIMITED

BEST/WORST/EXPECTED CASE ...

List of assumptions ....

Cashflow projections for the twelve month period ending 28 February 2011

v	Item													Total
	Employer's NIC				64	64	64	64	64	64	64	64	64	576
v	Telephone and fax			529			529			529			529	2,115
v	Postage & stationery	176	176	173	176	176	176	176	176	176	176	176	176	2,115
v	Travel expenses	59	59	59	59	59	59	59	59	59	59	59	59	705
v	Repairs & renewals	29	29	29	29	29	29	29	29	29	29	29	29	353
v	Computer consumables	47	47	47	47	47	47	47	47	47	47	47	47	564
v	Miscellaneous	118	118	113	118	118	118	118	118	118	118	118	118	1,410
v	Legal & professional fees	470	470	470	470	470	470	470	470	470	470	470	470	5,640
	Accountancy fees	160	160	160	160	160	160	160	160	160	160	160	160	1,920
	Insurance	100	100	100	100	100	100	100	100	100	100	100	100	1,200
	Overdraft interest	0	0	0	0	0	0	0	0	0	0	0	0	0
	Loan payments	0	0	0	0	0	0	0	0	0	0	0	0	0
	HP payments	750	750	750	750	750	750	750	750	750	750	750	750	9,000
	Bank charges	40	40	40	40	40	40	40	40	40	40	40	40	480
	Factoring charges	0	0	0	0	0	0	0	0	0	0	0	0	0
	VAT (Rec'd)/Paid			480			533			533				1,546
	TOTAL PAYMENTS	1,949	1,949	16,278	14,573	14,445	19,622	16,882	16,702	19,878	20,882	21,214	58,758	223,132
	NET INFLOW/(OUTFLOW)	3,051	-1,949	158,722	-14,573	-13,445	-19,622	-16,882	-15,952	-19,878	-20,882	-20,814	29,367	47,143
	Opening Bank Balance	0	3,051	1,102	159,824	145,251	131,806	112,184	95,302	79,350	59,473	38,591	17,777	0
	Closing Bank Balance	3,051	1,102	159,824	145,251	131,806	112,184	95,302	79,350	59,473	38,591	17,777	47,143	47,143

v = includes Value Added Tax

Note: *Example for illustration purposes only*

Appendix C: Example profit and loss forecast: Enkryptikon Limited

ENKRYPTIKON LIMITED BEST/WORST/EXPECTED CASE …

List of assumptions ….

Profit and loss projections for the twelve month period ending 28 February 2011

	2010										2011		Total
	March £	April £	May £	June £	July £	Aug £	Sept £	Oct £	Nov £	Dec £	Jan £	Feb £	£
CASH INFLOW:													
Sales	0	0	0	0	0	0	0	0	0	0	75,000	75,000	150,000
Cost of sales:													
Components	0	0	0	0	0	0	0	0	0	0	23,250	23,250	46,500
Other materials	0	0	0	0	0	0	0	0	0	0	6,000	6,000	12,000
Research staff salaries	0	0	10,000	10,000	10,000	12,000	12,000	12,000	12,000	16,000	16,000	16,000	126,000
Employer's NIC	0	0	1,280	1,280	1,280	1,536	1,536	1,536	1,536	2,048	2,048	2,048	16,128
	0	0	11,280	11,280	11,280	13,536	13,536	13,536	13,536	18,048	47,298	47,298	200,628
Gross (loss)/profit	0	0	-11,280	-11,280	-11,280	-13,536	-13,536	-13,536	-13,536	-18,048	27,702	27,702	-50,628
Overheads:													
Rent	0		1,000	1,000	1,000	1,000	1,000	1,000	1,000	1,000	1,000	1,000	10,000
Rates and water			300	300	300	300	300	300	300	300	300	300	3,000
Light, heat and power			100	100	100	100	100	100	100	100	100	100	1,000
Administration salaries			500	500	500	500	500	500	500	500	500	500	5,000
Employer's NIC			64	64	64	64	64	64	64	64	64	64	640
Telephone and fax	150	150	150	150	150	150	150	150	150	150	150	150	1,800
Postage and stationery	150	150	150	150	150	150	150	150	150	150	150	150	1,800
Travel expenses	50	50	50	50	50	50	50	50	50	50	50	50	600
Repairs and renewals	25	25	25	25	25	25	25	25	25	25	25	25	300
Computer consumables	40	40	40	40	40	40	40	40	40	40	40	40	480
Miscellaneous	100	100	100	100	100	100	100	100	100	100	100	100	1,200
Legal & professional fees	400	400	400	400	400	400	400	400	400	400	400	400	4,800
Accountancy fees	160	160	160	160	160	160	160	160	160	160	160	160	1,920
Insurance	100	100	100	100	100	100	100	100	100	100	100	100	1,200
	1,175	1,175	3,139	3,139	3,139	3,139	3,139	3,139	3,139	3,139	3,139	3,139	33,740

ENKRYPTIKON LIMITED

BEST/WORST/EXPECTED CASE ...

List of assumptions ....

Profit and loss projections for the twelve month period ending 28 February 2011

												Total
Finance costs:												
Overdraft interest	0	0	0	0	0	0	0	0	0	0	0	0
Loan interest	0	0	0	0	0	0	0	0	0	0	0	0
HP interest	300	300	300	300	300	300	300	300	300	300	300	3,600
Bank charges	40	40	40	40	40	40	40	40	40	40	40	480
Factoring charges	0	0	0	0	0	0	0	0	0	0	0	0
	340	340	340	340	340	340	340	340	340	340	340	4,080
Depreciation:												
Plant & equipment	200	200	200	200	200	200	200	200	200	200	200	2,400
Office & computer equipment	0	0	0	0	0	0	0	0	0	0	0	0
Motor vehicles	0	0	0	0	0	0	0	0	0	0	0	0
	200	200	200	200	200	200	200	200	200	200	200	2,400
Net profit/(loss)	-1,715	-1,715	-14,959	-14,959	-4,959	-17,215	-17,215	-17,215	-21,727	24,023	24,023	-90,848
Cumulative profit/(loss)	-1,715	-3,430	-18,389	-33,348	-65,522	-82,737	-99,952	-117,167	-138,894	-114,871	-90,848	-90,848

Note: Examle for illustration purposes only

Appendix D: PEST analysis: major macro-environmental factors

PEST analysis factors

Political factors

- legislative changes UK
- legislative changes EU
- international regulatory changes
- industry regulatory changes
- national government change
- local government change

Social factors

- changes in people's lifestyles
- changes in aspirations and expectations
- changes in education levels
- changes in buying habits
- changes in demographics
- changes in ethnic groups
- changes in attitudes and opinions
- movements in fashion
- celebrity role models

Economic factors

- changes in standards of living
- economic changes in UK
- economic changes internationally
- direct and indirect taxation rates
- interest rates
- effects of seasonality patterns
- state of UK economic cycle

Technological factors

- emergence of new technologies
- emergence of rival and substitute technologies
- (tele)communications changes
- stage of product's technological life cycle
- consumer buying mechanisms/technology
- technology legislation, such as biogenetics

Index